INVITATION
to MUSIC

by Elie Siegmeister

PREFACE BY VIRGIL THOMSON

Illustrated by Beatrice Schwartz

HARVEY HOUSE, INC.
Publishers
Irvington-on-Hudson, New York

HARVEY HOUSE, Inc., *Publishers*
Irvington-on-Hudson, New York

© *1961 by Elie Siegmeister*

Illustrations © *1961 by Harvey House, Inc., N.Y.*

Library of Congress Catalog Card Number: 61-15658

Manufactured in the United States of America

To my three young people,
Mimi, Nancy, and Hannah,
with love

Preface

There used to be a business we called "the Music Appreciation Racket." That was twenty-five and more years ago. It was I who had made up that dirty name for it; and for quite a number of years the name stuck. It was justified, too, since most of the text books for helping the young people of that time to understand classical music had been written by people who did not understand it very well themselves.

Nowadays that is all changed. I have been astonished, reading the present book, to discover how broadly Mr. Siegmeister has covered the materials and history of music without giving false information or making foolish remarks.

It has been possible for him to do this because he is a practical musician and a composer of large experience. He knows the things he is talking about. Consequently, he can be brief without being superficial, can cover a vast field speedily, and still not omit anything important.

The present book does not offer a complete musical education. It is an elementary book for non-professional students. But it will not give anyone false ideas, either. It is a good book. It gives a clear and resembling picture of Western music, past and present, as viewed from the United States of America in the second half of the twentieth century. Filling out that picture with detail could be anybody's delight for a term, or for a lifetime.

VIRGIL THOMSON

Contents

Prelude

The best way to learn about music is to listen to it. But mere listening is not enough. It is how you listen and what you listen for that are important.

Opportunities for hearing the widest range of music—not once but over and over again—are now available almost everywhere. And what a range! From Bach to cool jazz, from blues to Bartók, from medieval motets to Shostakovich—all these are accessible to you at the end of a tone arm.

The more one knows about a subject, whether it be football, atomic physics, foreign cars, or symphonies, the more interesting and enjoyable it becomes. Although many people hear music with "half an ear," it can filter into the mind and give pleasure even to those who listen idly. But listening to music with full concentration is a far more pleasurable kind of experience.

This book was written very much as a piece of music is written—by a composer, for the listener. It is simply an "invitation to music." Certaintly, it does not tell everything there is to know about the subject, nor will reading the book make you a musical expert. But I hope it will help to deepen your understanding of this art, and give you new pleasure in the music you hear.

Many people have helped with their kind advice and suggestions in the preparation of this book. I want to express appreciation to my wife, Hannah; to my friends and colleagues: at Hofstra College, New York, Dr. Donald M. Rowe, Herbert Beattie, Albert Tepper, and Charles Raymond Vun Kannon; to Robert Gross, Professor of Music at Occidental College, California; and to William Mayer, David Robbins, John Rounds, and Don Smithers.

Great Neck, New York   E.S.

1

Music All Around Us

Throughout the sweep of history and down to the present day, music has played an important role in man's experience.

For centuries, men have used music to help them at their work. In ancient Babylon, a musician played the horn while slaves dragged huge statues into place. In Russia, men chanted as they hauled barges on the Volga. In Africa today, a drummer accompanies every kind of labor — in the village, on the docks, in the fields.

The theater, too, has always made important use of music. Ancient Greek dramas and the plays of Shakespeare had musical accompaniments. Many Broadway plays, as well as television programs, use music to heighten the dramatic effect. Musicals are perhaps the most sought-after form of entertainment in America today.

Have you ever watched a film after the sound went dead? What a dreary thing a movie is with no sound! Hollywood producers would not spend huge sums for background scores if music were not essential to the enjoyment of most motion pictures.

Some people consider music a luxury, an impractical, unnecessary pleasure. But how poor life would be without it!

Through music we can express our deepest feelings — joy, sorrow, pleasure, or pain. Usually, we can explain how we feel; but often our emotions are so deep, so strong, or so complex that we just cannot put them into words.

3

At such moments, music seems to speak for us, saying what we cannot express. Perhaps this explains music's tremendous appeal to people through the ages.

Folk Music

No one knows how music began, but by all evidence men sang and played instruments before they could write. Long before there was such a person as a trained musician, people created love songs, dance songs, story songs (ballads), work songs, religious songs, and magical songs. People all over the world built instruments and invented tunes to play on them. Such spontaneous music of the people is called "folk music."

Whatever men have felt, thought, or done, they have put into their songs. Many years ago a Negro working in the sun thought of his loved ones, and sang:

Ex. 1   Nobody Knows de Trouble I Seen

No - bod - y   knows   de   trou - ble   I   seen...

On the Erie Canal a boatman made up this tune as he walked behind his mule on the towpath:

Ex. 2   The Erie Canal

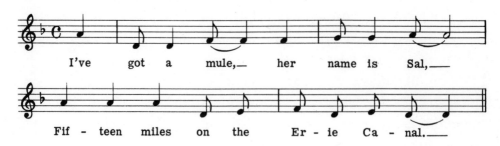

I've   got   a   mule,—   her   name   is   Sal,—

Fif - teen   miles   on   the   Er - ie   Ca - nal.—

4

A grizzled Forty-Niner, riding in his covered wagon across the Rockies, sang out his hopes and dreams in this way:

Ex. 3 Sacramento

Ho, boys,— ho! To Cal - i - for - nia go, There's plen-ty of gold in the world I'm told on the banks of Sac- ra - men-to.

The extent and the variety of the people's music are almost endless. Every nation has its own treasury of songs and of dance melodies, created by generations of unknown singers, fiddlers, banjo pickers, and players of other instruments. In this country alone, more than thirty thousand folk tunes have been collected in recent years. Yet these thousands are only a small part of the total number of folk melodies that man has created in the course of time.

The inventive powers of folk musicians are impressive. Without any formal knowledge of music, common people throughout the world have created a great variety of scales, rhythmic patterns, melodic styles, musical instruments, and ways of performing.

Unlike the music of trained composers, which is fixed in print, folk music is constantly changing. Each singer sings a tune in his own particular way. As the tune is repeated frequently over a period of years, the singer makes slight changes in words and music without being aware of doing so. Each change in itself may be very small, but after a time the many alterations in a song may eventually turn it into a completely new piece of music. When you realize that folk songs are passed along from father to son for many generations, you cannot be surprised that many different versions of a tune arise.

In 1665, the English author, Samuel Pepys, wrote in his famous diary that he heard a music-hall singer, Mrs. Knipps, sing the Scotch ballad, "Barbary Allen," in London. That song was brought over to the United States by our earliest settlers and was passed on by country people for almost three hundred years. A few years ago, a collector found ninety-eight different versions of "Barbara Allen" in the state of Virginia alone. Here are two of them:

Ex. 4 Barbara Allen

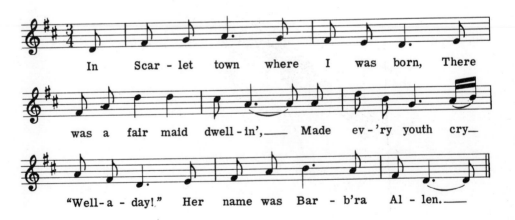

In Scar - let town where I was born, There
was a fair maid dwell - in', ___ Made ev - 'ry youth cry ___
"Well- a - day!" Her name was Bar - b'ra Al - len. ___

Ex. 5 Barbara Allen

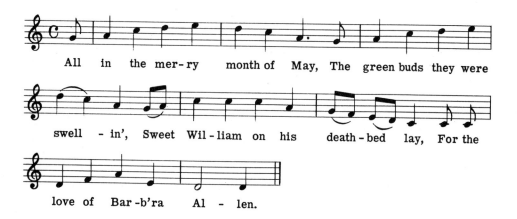

All in the mer-ry month of May, The green buds they were swell - in', Sweet Wil - liam on his death – bed lay, For the love of Bar -b'ra Al - len.

These two melodies have different rhythms: one is in 3/4, the other in 4/4 time. Their scales differ, the first being major, the second minor. The melodic lines are dissimilar. Yet these are but two of the many variations of the original "Barbary Allen" of 1665.

The Folk Musicians and the Composers

In their own way, many folk musicians are true artists. Such American folk singers as Leadbelly, Aunt Molly Jackson, and Woody Guthrie composed their own songs, each in his own personal fashion. Leadbelly's music is rough and hearty; Aunt Molly's has the harsh quality of the Kentucky Mountain mining camps. Guthrie's songs reflect the flat, dusty Oklahoma landscape where many of them were composed. The talent and imagination of thousands of such untaught country people have given the world its basic musical language—folk music.

Although the trained composer and the maker of folk songs live in different worlds, they share a common trait: a constant interest in new musical expression. Neither the composer nor the imaginative folk singer considers music a fixed language, but rather a world of new sound combinations waiting to be discovered.

Haydn, Tchaikovsky, Brahms, and Bartók loved folk music and often went to out-of-the-way places to hear it. Many of the songs they heard in villages and in fields turned up later as themes of symphonies, overtures, and operas.

Haydn used a Croatian folk song, "Oy Jellena," in his famous *London* Symphony. Here is the song in its original form, and also as it appears in Haydn's symphony:

Ex. 6 Croatian Folk Song, and Haydn: *London* Symphony

8

Tchaikovsky, like many other Russian composers, was fascinated by the peasant music of his country. The last movement of his Symphony No. 4 is based on the well-known Russian folk song, "The Birch Tree."

Ex. 7 The Birch Tree

Brahms, a serious, learned composer, loved the hearty songs of the German and Austrian countrysides. He made use of these songs in his overtures and choral music. One of the most delightful parts of his *Academic Festival* Overture is the folk song, "The Hunter from Kurpfalz."

Ex. 8 The Hunter from Kurpfalz

Let no one tell you that folk music is out of date. Some of the greatest modern composers have felt its vitality and used it in their compositions, just as musicians have done for hundreds of years. Stravinsky's most famous ballets, *The Fire Bird* and *Petroushka,* most of Villa-Lobos' works, and many compositions by Prokofiev, Milhaud,

Vaughan-Williams, Gershwin, Charles Ives, Aaron Copland, and Virgil Thomson were enriched by the use of folk songs and folk rhythms.

Ex.   9   Stravinsky: *Petroushka*

National Music

Every country has its own folk music. Just as great literature is rooted in the common language, so are the great forms of music based upon the simpler music of the people. In medieval Europe, various areas produced their individual styles of folk music. With the coming of nationalism, local and provincial styles gradually merged, forming a national music.

Many countries developed national melodies, rhythmic patterns, and styles of singing; some even created native instruments and characteristic ways of playing them.

In Spain, for instance, the music of the Spanish gypsies has its pulsing rhythms and wild melodies. The castanets, a native Spanish percussion instrument, are an essential feature of gypsy music. Spanish composers, such as Manuel de Falla, have woven the rhythms and phrases of this gypsy music into their compositions.

The music of Hungary, on the other hand, has a rugged, vigorous quality that dates back to the Magyars who settled in that country in the ninth century. The cimbalom is a traditional Hungarian stringed instrument played with small hammers. Zóltan Kodály, a present-day Hungarian composer, has introduced its individual sound into one of his orchestral scores, *Háry János*. Béla Bartók, another famous modern Hungarian composer, has based much of his music on the scales and rhythms

10

of peasant music. These two men are considered pioneers in the creation of a Hungarian musical style.

If we should examine the music of almost any country, from India to Mexico, we would find national music based on the traditions of its people. The great composers of the past have always had roots in their native soil, as do many composers living today.

Like styles in dress, food, or living habits, national styles in music have a way of crossing frontiers and becoming popular elsewhere than in the country of their origin. Over a hundred years ago the waltz, originally a German folk dance, journeyed from Vienna to Paris, then to America, and finally was the rage all over the world. A national music became international.

More recently, jazz, a particularly American product, crossed the seas in the opposite direction and is now, of course, almost as popular in Tokyo, Calcutta, and Odessa as it was in New Orleans fifty years ago.

A musical style that starts out by being national may become meaningful to men everywhere. Some day, perhaps Americans and Frenchmen will enjoy the music of India and China, just as many Indians and Chinese now enjoy the music of Gershwin and Debussy.

Fresco in the Vienna Opera House

2

What Music Is Made Of

The world of music is ancient and modern, wide and rich. It includes many different styles and forms of music. Think of the contrasts between a Sousa march and a reverent hymn; a hillbilly tune and an Italian opera; a rhumba and a Beethoven symphony!

Yet these types of music, which seem so different, all make use of the same basic materials.

What are the materials of music?

Just as wood, bricks, and mortar are needed to build a house, musical materials—among them melody, rhythm, tone color—are needed to make a musical composition. Of course, when the composition is completed, the materials are so blended that one rarely thinks of them separately. When you listen to one of your favorite compositions, whether it be Gershwin's *Rhapsody in Blue* or Mozart's *Eine Kleine Nachtmusik,* you enjoy it as a whole. You do not stop to say, "Ah! What an intricate harmony!" or, "What a delicious color contrast the muted trumpet makes against the soft strings!"

And yet a composition is often attractive precisely because of its rich harmony, its unusual tone color, or its fresh and surprising rhythm.

Some people are reluctant to examine music closely, to separate it into its various parts. They fear they may become entangled in technicalities and lose the simple pleasures of listening.

Do not be afraid to pause for a while and focus on the individual element. To penetrate the core of music is a challenge. By concentrating on one feature at a time, you sharpen your listening and deepen your understanding of music as a whole.

13

Now, let us look at the various materials of music: melody, rhythm, harmony, counterpoint, tone color, and form.

Melody

Melody is a primary material of music. It is the part of music that is easiest to listen to and to remember. Think of almost any composition, from "Dixie" to Beethoven's Fifth Symphony, and, most probably, you will be thinking of the melody.

A melody may be complete in itself. Certain kinds of music consist of melody only. Among them are folk songs, Gregorian chants, medieval troubadour songs and old German chorales. People sing, or whistle, popular songs and the themes of classical compositions, deriving pleasure solely from the tunes without accompaniment.

But, familiar as we are with the melodic part of music, it is difficult to say just what a melody is. Personally, I would rather write a melody than try to define one. If I were forced to give a definition, it might be somewhat like this: "Melody is a succession of tones arranged in an interesting or attractive pattern."

The trouble with such a definition is that it is full of holes. "Interesting" or "attractive," yes. But to whom? What is melodic to one person may be meaningless gobbledygook to another.

Here is a pattern of tones:

Ex. 10

To many people, this arrangement of tones would sound strange. Yet today, a group of musicians, known as "twelve-tone" composers, might find such an arrangement of notes quite acceptable as a melody.

14

Between these differing views, however, there is a middle ground on which people generally agree. Most of us would not fail to hear melody in the songs of Schubert, Mozart's operas, the symphonies of Beethoven and of Tchaikovsky, Gershwin's songs, and in the music of Debussy, Prokofiev, and Villa-Lobos.

Melody has the power to convey emotion, often revealing the most personal aspect of a composer's style. A simple pattern of tones, without the help of any harmony, can suggest gaiety, sadness, nobility, or strength.

Warmth and tenderness are found in this melody from Schubert's *Unfinished* Symphony:

Ex. 11   Schubert: Symphony No. 8 (*Unfinished*)

The minuet from Mozart's *Don Giovanni* has a melody which is all elegance and grace:

Ex. 12   Mozart: Minuet from *Don Giovanni*

There is simplicity and power in the march theme from Brahms' First Symphony:

Ex. 13   Brahms: Symphony No. 1

The variety of moods that can be created through melody alone is virtually endless. The unknown composer of "Go Down, Moses" conveyed through his song a feeling of noble, austere beauty:

Ex. 14 Go Down, Moses

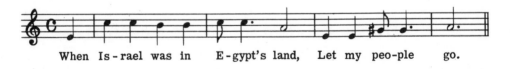

When Is - rael was in   E - gypt's land,   Let my peo - ple   go.

The exact nature of melody remains mysterious, but there is a well-known element that influences the structure of a melodic idea: the scale in which it is written.

Scale

Everyone has heard of scales, having learned and sung *do-re-mi-fa-sol-la-ti-do* in school. Not everyone, however, knows that the scale is one of the oldest inventions in music.

But even before the scale was invented, people sang melodies that followed certain scale patterns, although no one seemed aware of doing so.

Then, about three thousand years ago, discerning musicians began to notice that the same tone patterns occurred in many different melodies. Independently of each other, ancient musicians, Chinese and Greek, arranged these patterns in certain orders which we know as scales. Ever since, scales have been one of the foundations of music.

Why are scales important? Because the pattern of tones in a given scale guides and limits the course of a melody. If it were not for scales, melodies might roam wildly and get lost. A scale gives melody a definite orbit, in which it can move. When a melody leaves a scale, it can return to its home after the roaming is over.

To understand what comprises a scale, compare it with a staircase. If we start on "C," each tone of the scale would be a "step" up the "staircase"—eight steps in all. These eight steps form a series of tones called an "octave."

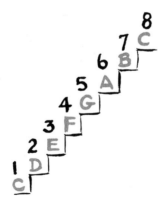

There is an important difference, however, between a scale and a flight of stairs. The steps of a staircase are all the same height, but in a scale, some steps are smaller than others. These small steps are known as "half steps," the larger ones "whole steps."

If the whole and half steps are arranged in a certain order, they form the major scale. As you can see, in this scale the half steps occur between the third and fourth tones, and likewise between the seventh and eighth.

Ex. 15 Major Scale

If the steps and half steps are arranged in another order, and an especially large step (a step and one half) is introduced between the sixth and seventh tones, a minor scale results.

Ex. 16 Minor Scale

Sing or play the major and minor scales and note the contrast in sound between the two.

Now, what difference does the position of a few half steps make? In music, as in many other things, of course, a slight difference can be very important. The particular positions of the half steps determine the sound of each scale and influence the music written in it.

18

Many people attribute special qualities to various scales. There is a popular belief that the major scale is happy, the minor scale sad.

Test this idea with a simple experiment. What would happen to a well-known tune if its scale were changed? Take "Three Blind Mice," which is in the major scale, and change it to the minor. You can do so by placing a flat (♭) before the third step of the scale, E, lowering it by a half tone.

Ex. 17 Three Blind Mice—Major and Minor

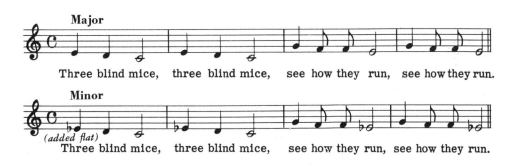

Whether or not the change from major to minor makes "Three Blind Mice" sad, everyone will agree that the song does sound *different*.

A change in scale in the middle of a composition may create a sharp change in mood—an effect often used by such composers as Schubert, Tchaikovsky, and Wagner. Beethoven made dramatic use of this procedure in his *Eroica,* or Third Symphony, when the main theme, originally in the major scale, suddenly appears in minor:

Ex. 18 Beethoven: *Eroica* Symphony

Belief in the emotional power of scales is very old. The ancient Greeks, for instance, considered a certain scale warlike, and, therefore, believed that music written in that scale would make men want to fight. Other scales were considered soft and sensuous, and hence unfit for the ears of young people.

Ludwig van Beethoven

20

An old Chinese legend tells of a musician who played the scale of winter in the middle of the summer. As a consequence, an icy wind blew down on the people and the rivers and lakes froze over. Those people certainly must have thought scales had tremendous powers. Perhaps they confused "musicians" with "magicians."

A scale may be called "a family of tones." This means that the eight tones in a given scale have a close relationship to each other, though they differ in rank and in importance. The fundamental tone is the first, or "tonic." It gives its name to a scale, as does a father to his family. You often hear the expression "the key of C." This means that a scale or key is built on C as the tonic. Similarly the key of B Flat is based on the tonic B Flat, and so on.

The tonic is the central point around which the other tones revolve. They circle about the central point freely for a time, then are drawn to it, as iron filings are attracted to a magnet. Most songs, after moving through a variety of tones, come to rest on the tonic at the end.

21

If you want to test the magnetic power of the tonic, sing "do-re-mi-fa-sol-la-ti," and stop. You have stopped on the seventh or "leading" tone of the scale — the tone that has a strong "urge" to move to the tonic. If you do not sing the next tone, anyone who is listening will say, "Finish it," thus testifying to the magnetic power of the tonic. This pull of the tonic is true only for the traditional major and minor scales.

Scales will be discussed further in Chapter 9.

How a Melody Moves

Granted that a melody is written in a particular scale, how does it move within the limits of that scale? Many melodies move by steps, up and down the scale, rising and falling smoothly from one tone to the next with an occasional small jump. This type of flowing motion is especially suited to vocal melodies.

Ex. 19   Au Clair de la Lune

Au clair de la lu - ne, mon am - i, Pier - rot.

Ex. 20   The First Noel

The First — No - el, the an - gel did say.

Melodies of this type have a smooth quality. They are calm, and easy to sing.

Other melodies, in which the notes leap about, have an active, vigorous feeling.

Ex. 21   Foster: De Camptown Races

Gwine   to   run   all   night,   Gwine   to   run   all   day,

Ex. 22   Beethoven: Symphony No. 9

The character of a melody is largely influenced by the quality of its motion, whether smoothly flowing, or jumpy and angular.

Most tunes written for singing have a span of eight to eleven tones, the range of the average voice. Operatic arias composed for trained singers, of course, have a wider compass.

Melodies, composed for an instrument, may range far and wide, up and down the scale, and move with great speed and complexity. Wide jumps and fast running notes, such as those found in Bach's Concerto in D Minor for two violins, would be impossible to sing, but easy to play on the violin or the piano.

Ex. 23   Bach: Concerto in D Minor for Two Violins

Melodic Curve

A good melody is like a fine drawing or painting. It has a definite shape or design. Musicians sometimes speak of a "melodic line" or "melodic curve."

The noted composer, Ernst Toch, has described various patterns of melodic curve. Some rise ⌒ ; others fall ⌐ . Still others move up and back around a central tone, making a "wave" motion ⌇⌇. There is a pattern called the "arch," ⌃ and its opposite one that forms a "bowl" ⌄

Here is a rising melody:

Ex. 24 Beethoven: Symphony No. 1

and here a falling one:

Ex. 25 Bizet: Habanera, from *Carmen*

This is a wave:

Ex. 26 Poor Wayfaring Stranger

I am a   poor— way - far - ing   stran - ger,— a - travel-ling

through this world of   woe.—

24

An arch:

Ex. 27 Beethoven: Violin Concerto in D Major

And a bowl:

Ex. 28 Handel: Joy to the World

Joy to the world! the Lord is come: Let earth re-ceive her King.

Many melodies start low, then rise in a series of waves, and reach a high point, or climax, near the end. The gradual upsweep to the highest peak carries feeling along with it, and makes an especially satisfying type of melodic curve. In Schubert's Waltz in A Flat, the melody rises from crest (↿) to crest, leading to the final climax (✳), after which the wave breaks.

Ex. 29 Schubert: Waltz in A Flat

Besides rising waves, there are also falling waves and other types of melodic curve.

When you listen to a song, you will find it interesting to follow the melody by "drawing" its curve, as shown in the example above.

To test your ability, see if you can draw the curve of the tunes given here. First sing the melody, then trace the curve of its opening part. Is it a rising or a falling line, an arch, a bowl, a wave, or a rising and falling wave? You will find the answers in Chapter 9.

1   "Drink to Me Only With Thine Eyes."
2   "The Minstrel Boy."
3   "On Top of Old Smoky."
4   "Jeanie With the Light Brown Hair."

Melodic Rhythm

Another important feature of a melody is its rhythm. Almost every tune you can think of has a definite rhythmic pattern. In some melodies the rhythm is so catchy that it is even more striking than the actual notes of the melody. Try tapping out the following rhythmic patterns with a pencil on a table top. Can you recognize the melodies to which they belong?

Ex.   30

For the answers, turn to Chapter 9.

Rhythm

Just what is rhythm? It is the pulsing or flowing of music in time. Important as melody is to music, rhythm is even more basic. As we have seen, many people find it difficult to think of music without melody. Yet in a number of preludes by Bach or Chopin, melody is of minor importance—the rhythm carries the music along.

When you are dancing, it is the beat, not the tune, that keeps you moving. When you are marching in a parade, no matter which tunes the trumpet or the piccolo plays, it is the ONE-two-three-four, ONE-two-three-four of the bass drum that helps you to keep step. On the old Yankee clippers, the heavily accented beat of the chanteyman's songs helped the sailors to pull together on the ropes at just the right moment:

> WHAT shall we do with the DRUNKen sailor,
> WHAT shall we do with the DRUNKen sailor,
> WHAT shall we do with the DRUNKen sailor,
> EARLye in the MORNing?

Rhythm moves us strongly not only because it is a part of music, but because it is a part of our life. The sun rises and sets; day follows night; the tides rise and recede in a regularly repeated pattern.

Music has taken its basic rhythms from those of the human body. The continuous pulsating beat of the heart is perhaps the most fundamental of all musical rhythms.

There is a certain kind of primitive dance music that consists of only the repeated beating of a drum. This primitive drumbeat is a series of notes spaced at equal intervals, somewhat like a heartbeat:

Ex. 31

But since a continuous series of steady beats can become monotonous, men soon found out that it is more interesting to sound one beat more loudly than others, or to "accent" it. (Accents are indicated in music by the sign >.)

Ex. 32

Originally, song, poetry, and the dance were closely related. In the dance, there is a tendency to move, turn, jump, or bring the foot up and down in regularly repeated patterns. In dance music the heavy, or accented beat, is usually the "downbeat," when the foot comes down.

To write the pattern of accented and unaccented beats, musicians invented the "measure" and the "bar-line." A measure, as here shown, is the unit of rhythm between two vertical bar-lines, with the accent usually, but not always, on the first beat.

Ex. 33

The bar-line came into use about 1600. In almost all European music from 1600 to about 1900 every measure in a composition contained the same number of beats. The signs, 2/4, 3/4, and 4/4 are symbols placed at the beginning of a composition to show how many beats there will be in each measure.

Here are examples of these common measures:

Ex. 34   Beethoven: Symphony No. 7

Ex. 35   Mozart: *The Marriage of Figaro*

Ex. 36   Good King Wenceslas

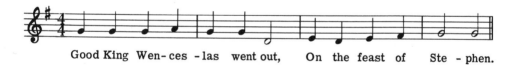

Rhythm would be a simple, but rather dull, affair if music consisted only of such elementary patterns. Actually, rhythm is much more interesting than that.

In popular dance music, for instance, there are often *two* rhythmic currents running at the same time. One is the underbeat, pulsing away steadily, usually in the bass or drums. The second rhythm is in the melody. This is a changing rhythm, with notes of varying lengths. One note may last two or more beats; there may be several notes to a single beat; and the rhythm may change from measure to measure. The varying rhythm gives added interest to the melody.

The "Merry Widow Waltz," by Franz Lehar, has the bass (in this case the left hand on the piano) playing the steady "UM-pah-pah" underbeat of all waltzes:

Ex. 37 Lehar: Merry Widow Waltz—Left Hand

Over the bass, the right hand plays the melody, with its varied rhythms. For four measures, there are long and short notes, then longer notes end the phrase.

Ex. 38 Lehar: Merry Widow Waltz—Right Hand

If we put the music for the right and the left hands together, the way the composer wrote it, we can see a difference between the varied melodic rhythm and the fixed, throbbing underbeat:

Ex. 39 Lehar: Merry Widow Waltz

30

It is mainly in dance music, in marches and in simple songs that the underbeat is insistent. And even here, a good dance band will know how to give the feeling of a steady beat, while varying it to avoid monotony.

In most classical music, however, the bass does not hammer away at the underbeat. The beat is there, but often it is only felt, not heard, as in the following:

Ex. 40   Chopin: Prelude in A

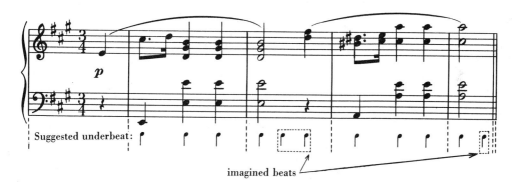

Not all the beats are actually played in this composition. The left-hand underbeat rhythm is established in the first measure. In measures two and four, the listener supplies the missing beats in his imagination. In this way the composer lets "air" into his music. He also calls on the listener to be creative, to supply part of the music in his own mind.

This is one reason why it requires more experience and a more vivid imagination to follow classical music than it does to follow popular music.

I have given you only a few elementary aspects of rhythm. It requires a great deal of musical experience to be aware of the intricate rhythms of both popular and classical music. The ability can be acquired by listening to music in which rhythm is an important factor, and by trying to figure out what the composer does, rhythmically speaking.

31

Note, for instance, the steady, vigorous rhythms of a Handel suite or a Bach fugue. Listen to the powerful rhythms of Beethoven's Fifth Symphony, or the wild, exhilarating ones of his Seventh Symphony. The last movement of Mendelssohn's *Italian* Symphony has the giddy, whirling movement of a tarantella, and some of Chopin's preludes and mazurkas drive along at a furious pace. The Revolutionary Scene in Moussorgsky's opera, *Boris Godunov,* has the relentless rhythms of an aroused people.

The rhythmic power and inventiveness of the Classical composers added much to the vitality of their music. Yet, inventive as they were, most European composers of the Classical period wrote mainly in what we term "regular" rhythms. They were limited by what musicians sometimes call "the tyranny of the bar-line."

Regular rhythms are those in which the underbeat and the melody, different as they may be in rhythmic details, fit together neatly in their basic patterns. In Brahms' *Hungarian Dance* No. 5, for example, the accents of the underbeat and the melody come together regularly on the first beat of each measure.

Ex. 41   Brahms: Hungarian Dance No. 5 (adapted)

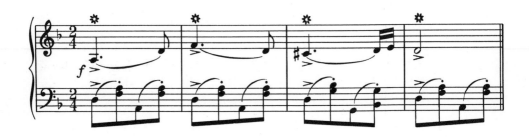

The sign, *, in Ex. 41, indicates where the regular rhythms fit together.

32

Cross-Rhythms

Before the twentieth century most of the known music came from Europe. But, nowadays, it is common knowledge that Asia, Africa, and America have created fascinating and distinctive musical styles of their own. These styles differ from traditional European music, among other ways, by the use of more complex rhythmic patterns, such as cross-rhythms. In cross-rhythmic music the melody follows one rhythmic pattern, 4/4 perhaps, while the underbeat forms a different one, such as 3/8. Here is a modern American example of cross-rhythm:

Ex. 42 Siegmeister: Three Preludes

The two rhythms are completely independent of each other. Note that the accents in right and left hands are played together only at the beginning. Afterwards, they come at different times, causing a rhythmic clash.

For some people cross-accented rhythm may be difficult to play. But cross-rhythms of this type are heard every day in such places as Bombay, Bali, and Baltimore.

In the twentieth century, leading European composers discovered the exciting rhythms of Africa and Asia, and introduced them into modern European music for the first time. The combination of European melody and harmony, with African and Asian cross-rhythms, in such

33

works as Stravinsky's *The Rite of Spring,* Milhaud's *The Creation of the World,* and Bartók's string quartets, opened a dazzling new period in music.

Syncopation

In the 1920's, American musicians also discovered the complex and fascinating African cross-rhythms. These were brought to America in the days of the slave trade, and were kept alive in the music of Southern Negroes. The offbeat, clashing rhythms of Negro folk music are illustrated in the old spiritual, "Didn't My Lord Deliver Daniel?"

Ex. 43   Didn't My Lord Deliver Daniel?

Syncopation occurs when an offbeat is strongly accented, or when, as shown in the above example, a strongly accented melody note falls *between* the regular beats. The conflict between the offbeat accent in the melody and the regular accents in the bass produces the rhythmic zest of American Negro folk music and of much popular music as well. Jazz has developed the art of crisscrossing rhythms—also called poly-rhythms—to a high degree.

Although European composers have made rich use of syncopation and rhythmic conflict, these techniques have been still further developed by such American composers as Charles Ives, Gershwin, Copland, Gould, and Bernstein, and by the Latin-Americans, Revueltas and Villa-Lobos. Rhythmic invention has added much to the sparkle and vitality of all forms of American music.

Tempo

In a discussion about rhythm one often hears the word "tempo" mentioned. Tempo refers to the rate of speed at which a piece of music is played. People speak of a fast tempo, a slow tempo, a moderate tempo, changes of tempo, and so on.

The character of a piece can be altered by changing the speed of its performance. A composer builds excitement by increasing the tempo; he produces a feeling of relaxation by slowing it down. Many subtle effects are created by a performer when he plays in *tempo rubato*—a tempo in which certain notes of the melody are speeded up or slowed down, while the music as a whole maintains a steady pulse.

Indications of tempo are usually given in Italian, the international language of music. Here are some used most frequently.

Presto—very fast
Allegro—fast
Allegretto—moderately fast
Moderato—moderately
Andante—moving along, but slowly
Adagio—slow
Largo—very slow
Accelerando—getting faster
Animando—getting faster
Ritenuto—held back, slower
Ritardando—getting slower
Allargando—getting broader (slower)

Harmony

In primitive and ancient times, and probably for thousands of years, music consisted of melody and rhythm only. It is believed that when people made music in groups, everyone played—or tried to play—the same tones, with, at most, some kind of drumbeat or other rhythmic accompaniment. No one had discovered the pleasure of playing different sounds at the same time.

About 850 A.D., man took the first step toward creating the new musical idiom we call harmony. A primitive type of harmony, the drone, is known to many peoples. It is a long, deep tone sustained under a melody, as in the music of the Scotch bagpipe.

A slightly more advanced kind of harmony developed when two or more people sang a song, one singing the melody on a higher pitch than the other. This procedure added resonance, or enriched quality, to the original melody.

36

37

Simple methods of blending tones were developed by many peoples, but harmony, in its full sense, did not come into being until some time after the year 1200, when the musicians of medieval Europe invented chords. Music that consists of melody with chord accompaniment is called "homophonic."

We have already learned that melody is a series of tones sounded one after the other. A chord is a group of tones sounded at the same time. For example, take the first notes of an old Negro spiritual:

Ex. 44   Roll, Jordan, Roll

Sound them together:

Ex. 45   C Major Chord

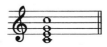

This is the most common chord in all music, the so-called C major chord. If this chord is played on the piano with the left hand an octave lower than it is written here, several different melodies may be played over it with the right hand. The result is quite pleasing. Play the following melodic phrases, accompanied by the C major chord in the left hand:

Ex. 46   Foster: De Camptown Races

If a flat is added to the E in the C major chord, it becomes a minor chord:

Ex. 47   Major Chord

Ex. 48   Minor Chord

(added flat)

As with scales, minor chords seem darker and more solemn than major ones—though there are exceptions to this, as to all general statements about music!

Chords sounded along with a melody add richness and serve as a background, very much as a stage setting adds atmosphere and serves as a background to the actors in a play.

In this phrase from Schubert's "Serenade," notice how the melody is supported and enriched by the harmonic background—accompaniment.

Ex. 49 **Schubert: Serenade (adapted)**

Remove the background of chords and you rob the music of its third dimension. The melody, lovely as it is, seems to hang suspended, without foundation:

Ex. 50 **Melody from Schubert's Serenade (adapted)**

Harmony, however, is not merely an added color in the background. In most of the compositions written between 1600 and 1900, harmony has given music its foundation and inner structure. Many melodies have harmonies built into them. Thus, the opening of the well-known slow movement theme of Haydn's *Surprise* Symphony is really nothing more than two chords, in which the notes are sounded one after another, instead of being struck together.

Ex. 51 **Haydn: *Surprise* Symphony**

Besides its relation to melody, harmony has several qualities of its own that are quite interesting. Chords give color to, and create a mood in, music. Some chords are clear and transparent, like this one:

Ex. 52   Chord in High Register, Open Position

Other chords are dark and rich, like this one:

Ex. 53   Chord in Low Register

No composer was more gifted in establishing a dramatic atmosphere through the use of harmony than Richard Wagner. In two of his most famous operas, *Tristan and Isolde* and *The Mastersingers of Nuremberg,* he sets the mood in the very first chords. Here are the beautiful opening harmonies of *Tristan and Isolde.* Complex and tense, they immediately evoke the brooding, restless mood that is to be developed throughout the whole work:

Ex. 54   Wagner: *Tristan and Isolde*

41

What a contrast to *Tristan and Isolde* are the opening chords of *The Mastersingers*! Robust, open, and sunny, the chords reveal immediately the straightforward character of the work that is to follow. Wagner used the C major chord, the most common one in all music, to suggest these hearty, though tradition-bound, German townspeople.

Ex. 55 Wagner: *The Mastersingers of Nuremberg*

Certain composers, notably Monteverdi, Beethoven, Chopin, Wagner, Debussy, and Schönberg, were pioneers in harmony. They developed new chords, used old chords in daring new ways, and influenced the harmonic writing of the musicians who followed them.

In modern times, many new chords have been added that have changed the whole feeling of music. When you listen to a composition, whether old or modern, you can gain much pleasure by paying special attention to the harmonies that support the melodic line.

The discussion of harmony is continued in Chapters 7 and 9.

Counterpoint

Some people are frightened by the word, "counterpoint." In their opinion, counterpoint is music for experts only. When they hear a composition with more than one melodic line, they close their ears and dismiss it as too difficult.

Listening to Bach certainly requires more concentration than listening to Irving Berlin. But to many listeners—even those who have never studied music—the works of Bach and other contrapuntal composers are among the finest compositions ever written and well worth the effort to understand them.

If you look it straight in the eye, you will recognize counterpoint as an old friend. You have probably sung rounds such as "Row, Row, Row Your Boat." Counterpoint is like a round: it consists of different voices or instruments, each performing its own independent melody, each starting at just the right moment, with all parts fitting neatly together. Counterpoint is the art of combining separate and independent melodic lines into a composition.

For an interesting experiment, bring together three or four people to sing "Frère Jacques." Notice how the different voices enter, one after the other, each singing the melody at his appointed time; and how all blend together, making an interesting musical pattern.

Ex. 56 Frère Jacques

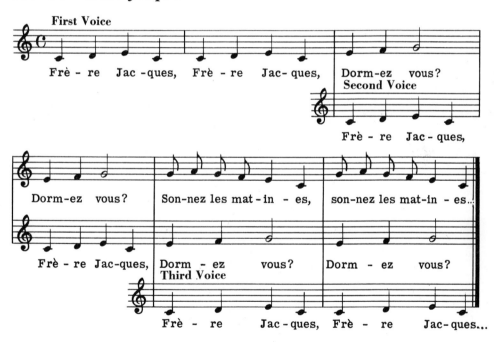

The nature of contrapuntal or "polyphonic" music becomes clear when we compare it with homophonic music. In homophonic music the top voice, or melody, stands out, with the other voices forming the background. When music is written in counterpoint, however, all the voices are equally important. Each has its own independent part and the voices are constantly interweaving, with now one and now another taking the leading position.

Look at this piece of homophonic music, Rameau's *Le Tambourin*. Here, the upper voice has the starring role, while the other voices act as supporting players.

Ex. 57   Rameau: Le Tambourin

Now let us examine a piece of counterpoint, Bach's Two Part Invention in F Major. When you play or listen to it you will notice that (as in the round, "Frère Jacques") the first voice starts the melody. Then a second voice takes it up in "imitation."

Ex. 58   Bach: Two Part Invention in F Major

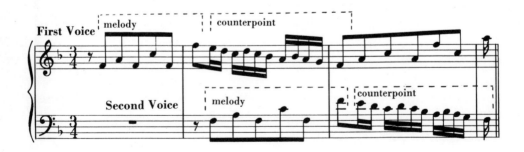

44

Facsimile of Portion of Bach's Manuscript Page, "Well-Tempered Clavichord"

This is true counterpoint, because neither voice is more important than the other; both have equal roles. Just as in a round, the two voices in the invention never do the same thing at the same time. At any one particular moment, the two voices are moving independently of each other. The invention is but one of the forms of contrapuntal music, some of which, like the fugue, are quite complex.

For a discussion of the fugue, see Chapter 9.

Counterpoint is one of the basic techniques used by classical composers, and by many jazz musicians, as well. Listen to a symphony orchestra or to a modern band. At times, each instrument seems to be going its own way. It is like a crossword puzzle for the ear. However, once you have learned how to follow the different voices in a contrapuntal work—a fugue by Bach, a string quartet by Mozart, or a jazz improvisation—you will have discovered a new source of musical pleasure.

Tone Color

When a composer has written a melody and harmonized it, his work is not necessarily completed. He must often decide which instruments will play his music—in other words, what tone colors to use.

Tone color, also known as "timbre," is one of the important materials used by the composer. In this field he has a wide choice. He can brighten his music with sounds of the flute or trumpet, or darken it, with those of the bassoon or double bass. He can use harsh and piercing tones (for example, a xylophone played loudly) or round, mellow tones (a French horn or cello).

A sensitive composer uses timbre in the same way a fine artist uses color. He may prefer sounds that blend to create a smooth, unified quality, like harmonious colors in a painting.

Contemporary painters, such as Matisse or Picasso, prefer startling colors that clash. They may place orange next to pink, perhaps with a dash of purple or yellow between the two. Like the painters, modern composers bring together timbres of very different kinds. Stravinsky has written a work, *The Story of a Soldier,* for violin, double bass, clarinet, bassoon, trumpet, trombone and drums. The different tone colors of these instruments are sharply set off against one another in this work. Many people find such tonal combinations wonderfully fresh and exciting.

The art of selecting and combining instrumental colors is known as "orchestration." To a good orchestrator, the variety of color combinations in music is almost endless. Imagine "Oh, Susanna" played by four flutes—it would have a light, delicate quality. Now think of it played by four trombones—the effect would be brassy and vigorous. What a brittle, crackling sound would come out of four xylophones hammering out the Foster tune! It is apparent that the character of a composition changes with the use of different tone colors.

Are you able to recognize the sounds of various instruments when you hear them in the orchestra? To test your ability, listen to recordings of the following compositions and name the first instrument you hear in each:

46

1   Debussy—*The Afternoon of a Faun*
2   Schubert—Symphony No. 7 in C Major
3   Gershwin—*Rhapsody in Blue*
4   Gershwin—Concerto in F
5   Schubert—Symphony No. 8 *(Unfinished)*
6   Tchaikovsky—Symphony No. 4 (second movement)
7   Brahms—Symphony No. 4
8   Moussorgsky-Ravel—*Pictures at an Exhibition*
9   Stravinsky—*The Rite of Spring*
10   Stravinsky—*Fire Bird* Suite

For the correct names, see Answers to Questions, in Chapter 9.

Dynamics

Tone color is altered not only by a change of instrument, but also by a change of method in playing the same instrument. A composition that is usually played softly sounds quite different when it is played loudly. The markings indicating the quantity of tone are called "dynamics." Dynamics are always shown in Italian words, spelled-out or abbreviated:

piano, or *p*	soft
pianissimo, or *pp*	very soft
mezzo forte, or *mf*	medium loud
forte, or *f*	loud
fortissimo, or *ff*	very loud

Pitch

Pitch, also, affects tone color. Test this by playing any tune, "Yankee Doodle," for instance, on the highest notes of the piano. What a thin, tinkly sound those notes make!

Ex. 59   Yankee Doodle (Treble)

Now try the same piece on the lowest notes of the keyboard. The result is a thick, heavy effect.

Ex. 60   Yankee Doodle (Bass)

Obviously, the melody is the same, whether it is played in high or in low range. Then what has caused the difference in sound?

It is "pitch" that has caused the difference.

Pitch is the name for the position of a tone in the musical scale. High pitches—the upper tones of a violin or a soprano voice—sound bright and clear. Low pitches—those produced by the bottom notes of the tuba or the bass voice—are dark and often ponderous.

Some people consider the very highest and the very lowest tones unpleasant. This may be true on occasion, but when they are used well they are effective and colorful. Think of *Peter and the Wolf*. Here the top notes of the flute portray the bird at the top of the tree, and the lowest notes of the bassoon depict the grumbling old grandfather.

48

If you are curious about what causes the difference between high and low pitch, open the top of a piano and look inside. You will notice that to the right—toward the high range of pitch—the strings become short and thin. To the left, toward the low tones, the strings grow long and thick. The length of the string and its thickness or thinness help determine its rate of vibration when struck. The more frequent the vibrations, the higher the pitch. The vibrations determine whether you will hear the sound as a high note or a low note, or a note in the middle range.

The same principle is true of other instruments. The violin, which plays the highest tones of all the string instruments, has the shortest, lightest strings. The double bass has long, heavy strings to make the deepest sounds. The piccolo, the smallest of the wood-wind instruments, plays the highest tones; the bassoon needs its long tube to produce the deepest notes of the wood-wind section.

Later on, in Chapter 5, we shall examine the tone colors of the various instruments of the orchestra.

Form

Melody, tone color, rhythm, and harmony are the materials of music; form is the way they are put together to make a unified whole. Without form, music would wander aimlessly, and become a shapeless patchwork of ideas. As an example of how music might sound without form, here is a musical hodgepodge in which bits and snatches of various tunes are pasted together:

Ex. 61

Lul -la - by and good night, The old grey mare, she ain't what she used to be, Lost my part - ner, Skip to my Lou, Let my peo - ple go.

It is easy to recognize form in objects we can see.

The church shown here has form—a round window in the center is flanked by two towers. As the eye travels from left to right, it sees a vertical line (left tower), a circular shape (the window) and a repetition of the vertical line (right tower). The line, the circle, and the repeated line make a balanced structure that gives pleasure to the eye.

Can one also recognize form in the sound of music? Listen to an old nursery tune:

Ex. 62 Twinkle, Twinkle Little Star

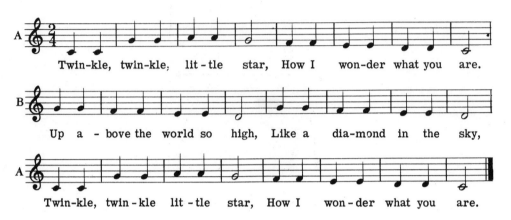

A — Twin-kle, twin-kle, lit-tle star, How I won-der what you are.

B — Up a - bove the world so high, Like a dia-mond in the sky,

A — Twin-kle, twin-kle lit-tle star, How I won-der what you are.

If you examine this tune, you will find it has three lines, or phrases, of music. The lines of the first (A) and the last (A) are alike, as are the two towers of the church. In the center there is a different phrase (B), which contrasts with the two (A) lines in the same way as the round window in the church contrasts with the two towers.

Because the song has form, it makes sense, is easy to remember, and appeals to the listener. Music that has no form produces a vague, confused, and unsatisfied feeling.

The form of "Twinkle, Twinkle, Little Star" is known in music as the ABA, or Three Part form. It is a form found in thousands of folk tunes and popular songs, as well as in classical compositions.

The recognition of form in music depends largely on memory. In looking at a painting, you see the whole form at once, the details later. In music, however, you hear the details—the individual melodies or phrases—first. Only by remembering all the phrases of a song or a larger work, and then adding them together, do you become aware of the total musical form.

52

The Motive

What happens when a composer sits down to write a piece of music? He generally thinks for a while, or he plays the piano, and soon he finds a short group of notes that interests him. Such a group of notes, when used to build a composition, is called a "motive."

Many years ago, an English song writer, Henry Carey, invented this motive:

Ex. 63   (Motive)

"Well, that's fine," he may have said to himself, "but what do I do now?" for a motive by itself is hardly a song. Mr. Carey tried repeating his motive, starting a little higher on the keyboard.

Ex. 64

Now he was beginning to accomplish something, but he knew the piece was not finished. Then he added a closing bit:

Ex. 65

53

Put these measures together and the result sounds quite familiar:

Ex. 66

Of course, what Mr. Carey did not know was that the melody he was writing would some day become the tune of one of our great national songs, "America." At any rate, having arrived that far, he had finished the first phrase, or Part, of the song. If we continue,

Ex. 67

we discover that Mr. Carey "inverted" the first motive, or turned it upside down, to make the second Part—which is a balance for the first Part. This song is an example of a Two Part form.

Two and Three Part Forms

In composing one may start with a short motive, develop it into a phrase and then into a whole song. The song will usually have either Two Parts (A-B) or Three Parts (A-B-A). About nine-tenths of all traditional and popular tunes, and a great number of classical compositions as well, are written in either of these two forms.

Think of some familiar melodies and try to find out whether they have Two or Three Parts. You can recognize the end of a Part by a pause in the music, where it seems to take a breath before continuing.

Here is a list of familiar songs. Which of these are Two Part, and which are Three Part?

"Pop Goes the Weasel"
"My Bonnie Lies Over the Ocean"
"Old Man River"
"Yankee Doodle"
"Old Folks at Home"

See Answers to Questions in Chapter 9.

Notice that in some songs, such as "Oh, Susanna," the first phrase is sung twice at the very beginning, giving the pattern A-A-B-A. Because the repetition of A only emphasizes the first Part, without introducing any new phrase, the A-A-B-A form is still considered a Three Part form.

Ex. 68   Foster: Oh, Susanna

I— came from A - la - bam - a wid my ban - jo on my knee,

I'm goin' to Louis-i - an - a,   my__   true love for to   see.

Oh! Su - san - na! Oh, don't you cry for me,

I've come from A - la - bam-a wid my ban-jo on my knee.

If you listen to Beethoven's Ninth Symphony, you will find the same A-A-B-A form in the famous "Ode to Joy" section.

Ex. 69   Beethoven: Ode to Joy, from Symphony No. 9

Although most well-known songs are composed in the familiar Two and Three Part forms, there are a great many very beautiful melodies that do not fit into these clear, symmetrical patterns. Hundreds of lesser-known folk songs and melodies by classical composers have irregular, free forms that are refreshing and distinctive. Songs such as the old Christmas carol, "God Rest You Merry, Gentlemen," are interesting examples of free form. Notice that this song has five phrases, in the pattern A-A-B-C-C, and that the last phrase is shorter than the others. This irregularity of form gives the melody a fresh quality.

Ex. 70   God Rest You Merry Gentlemen

We have examined some of the forms found in traditional and popular songs. These, of course, are among the simplest forms we know. As music developed, its patterns gradually became richer and more complex. In the following pages we shall see how, in the course of hundreds of years, the great forms of vocal and instrumental music have emerged.

3

The Great Forms of Music

Instrumental Forms

Modern Europe made a significant contribution to the world of art by creating the great forms of instrumental music. Other civilizations have produced magnificent poetry, drama, painting, sculpture, and architecture, but only Europe has given the world the sonata, the concerto, the symphony, and other great forms of instrumental music.

The Suite

The suite is one of the oldest of the great musical forms. Its origins date back to European folk dance music of over three hundred years ago. Old-time dances, such as the minuet, the gavotte, the jig, and the horn-pipe, were invented and played by peasants long before people in cities heard them.

Then, these dances were brought to Vienna, Paris, and other big cities—just as the rhumba, the mambo, and the cha cha were recently brought from Latin America to the United States. It became the custom for orchestras to play dance melodies in a group. This group, or "suite" of dances, was established as a form of popular entertainment music in the sixteenth century.

Later, skilled composers, Couperin, Purcell, Bach, and Handel among them, were attracted to the suite, and adopted it as their own. They developed the form until it gained in richness and depth. Bach and Handel wrote suites for single instruments, such as the piano or the cello, as well as for orchestra. Each movement in a Bach suite has its own dance rhythm—the bourrée, gavotte, polonaise and others. Generally, classical suites contained from four to eight movements.

Ex. 71 Handel: Hornpipe, from *Water Music*

Today a suite does not necessarily consist of dance music. A modern suite is a group of pieces in contrasting moods, wherein all the movements are musically related. Nineteenth and twentieth century suites often suggest a story or reflect a scene—*Scheherazade* by Rimsky-Korsakoff, *Ibéria* by Debussy, and my own *Sunday in Brooklyn.* A suite may also be a new arrangement, for concert performance, of music

Edvard Grieg

originally written for a ballet, a theater production, or a film. Tchaikovsky's *Nutcracker* Suite, Grieg's *Peer Gynt* Suite, and Prokofiev's *Lieutenant Kijé* are examples.

Ex. 72 Tchaikovsky: Russian Dance from *Nutcracker* Suite

The Rondo

The "rondo" was originally a folk dance in which people danced round and round in a circle. Then it became a short piece of dance music used in the suite. Eventually, it developed into one of the large forms used by Haydn, Beethoven, and many other composers. The rondo form allows the composer who has found a melody to repeat it several times without monotony.

In the rondo, each appearance of the main theme is followed by a contrasting theme. The main theme then returns, followed by another contrasting theme, and so on.

If A stands for the main theme, and B, C, D for contrasting themes, the scheme of the rondo is A B A C A D A. Listen to a well-known rondo such as Mozart's Rondo *Alla Turca* and see if you can make a plan of its main and its secondary themes.

Ex. 73   Mozart: Rondo *Alla Turca,* from Sonata in A Major

The Sonata

If you study piano, violin, cello or flute, at some time or other you will be given a rather long, impressive composition called a "sonata." At first, the word simply meant "a piece that sounds." But later on the sonata became, like the suite, a composition for one or two instruments in several movements, usually three or four.

The first and most important movement of the sonata is in so-called "sonata form." Do not confuse the sonata, which is the work as a whole, with "sonata form," which is the pattern of one or more of its movements.

A melody or "theme," often stormy and vigorous, introduces the first movement of the sonata. A contrasting second theme, usually song-

Wolfgang Amadeus Mozart

like and tender, follows. There may be more than two themes, and occasionally as many as four or five, each one possessing a strongly marked character. When all the themes have been heard, the "exposition," as it is called, is completed.

Next comes the "development," an interesting and complex section. In the development, parts of the themes previously heard are brought back, but generally in disguised form. Here the composer reveals his imagination and skill in the handling of materials. A development, at times, may be highly dramatic. Themes are broken into fragments; they interrupt one another, and there are many clashes and surprises. At the end of the development, a climax is reached.

The third section is called the "recapitulation." Once again, the themes presented at the beginning are heard, perhaps in slightly varied form. The recapitulation marks the end of the first movement.

The second movement of the sonata is usually slow, songlike and expressive. It may be in Three Part form or rondo form, and is frequently less complex in structure than is the first movement. If the sonata consists of four movements, the third is generally a lively, rhythmic minuet or scherzo—a brisk, dancelike movement, which may have touches of humor or sudden changes of mood.

The last movement of a sonata, almost always, runs fast and spiritedly. It may be either in rondo or in sonata form.

Sonatas contain some of the most magnificent music ever written for single instruments. If you have never heard a sonata, you should hasten to the nearest library that has a record collection and ask to hear Mozart's Piano Sonata in C Major (K. 545) or his lovely A Major Sonata (K. 331). Beethoven's *Moonlight* Sonata is world famous, but do not fail to listen to his stormy Sonata *Pathetique,* opus 13,

Ex. 74   Beethoven: Sonata *Pathetique*

and the magnificent Sonata *Appassionata,* opus 57. After you have heard the beautiful clarinet sonatas of Brahms, you can start on some modern violin or flute sonatas by Milhaud, Hindemith, Prokofiev, and Ives.

Eighteenth Century Chamber Music Group

The sonata pattern is not confined to music for one or two instruments. When a sonata is written for three or more players, it is called a trio, a quartet, a quintet, or a sextet, depending on the number of instruments used. When a sonata is written for a large orchestra, it is called a symphony.

Chamber Music Forms

In the courts of the German and Austrian nobility, some two hundred years ago, it was customary for the servants to double as performers on musical instruments. The cooks, gardeners, and coachmen, besides playing solos and duets for the master's entertainment, also performed in trios (three players), quartets (groups of four), and quintets (five players). The most popular combination was that of two violins, a viola, and a cello—the so-called string quartet.

Music played in the nobleman's room or chamber took on the name, "chamber music." The first string quartets, designed for light entertainment, were mostly elegant and charming. Heard in a small room, this

music was very delicate and pretty. Later on, the masters of chamber music, Mozart, Haydn, and Beethoven, made the string quartet into a serious, complex and expressive form. Beethoven's seventeen quartets contain some of his most personal and deeply moving music. Schubert, Brahms, Bartók, and Shostakovich also wrote some of their finest works in the form of chamber music.

Chamber music is a subtle and intimate art. Unlike orchestral music, which often makes its effects through massive contrasts, chamber music appeals to us through delicate means. Because of its subtlety, such music demands repeated hearings. But when you begin to understand it, chamber music may well become your favorite.

Ex. 75 Beethoven: String Quartet Op. 18, No. 1

The Symphony

The symphony is the most modern of the large musical forms. In the symphony, many outstanding composers of the past two centuries have expressed their deepest emotions and thoughts. A symphony is like a great drama—it has breadth and sweep. More than just music to give pleasure or to delight the ear, the symphony may also carry the composer's comment on life as a whole, presenting his vision of the world.

In its early beginnings, about 1750, the symphony was a short work written for a small group of musicians who performed in a nobleman's salon. The eighteen or twenty players who formed the orchestra in those days were really a large chamber music group.

Many of the lovely symphonies of Haydn and Mozart were written for such an intimate orchestra. They reflect the elegance and grace of the court.

Ex. 76 Mozart: Minuet from *Jupiter* Symphony, No. 41

In Beethoven's time, as music was performed more frequently in public concerts, the orchestra grew in size and richness. New instruments were added, and the symphony began to achieve great power.

Of course, not every symphony is powerful or dramatic. There are different kinds of symphonies. Some are light and tuneful, such as Mozart's *Haffner* Symphony and Haydn's *Surprise* Symphony. Some are symphonies for fun, such as Prokofiev's Classical Symphony. Beethoven's *Pastorale* Symphony is light-hearted, breathing the air of the country. There are even symphonies that make use of jazz motives, such as Aaron Copland's *Dance* Symphony.

But the most impressive of all symphonies are those that express the human drama, the struggle of man against fate. Examples of this type of symphony are: Schubert's *Unfinished,* Tchaikovsky's Sixth, Brahms' First, Prokofiev's Fifth, and Shostakovich's Tenth.

The first and, possibly, still the greatest of composers to introduce dramatic and philosophic problems into the symphony was Beethoven. His Fifth Symphony remains one of the most important treatments in music of man's struggle against fate. Here are its famous opening measures:

Ex. 77   Beethoven: Symphony No. 5

Beethoven's Third Symphony, the *Eroica,* suggests the glory and tragedy of a great man. Perhaps the most dramatic of all symphonies is his famous Ninth.

In the first three movements of this beautiful work, Beethoven created the feeling of noble tragedy. To bring the symphony to a fitting

Mendelssohn in His Twelfth Year

climax, the composer used not only instrumental music, but also vocal music—a striking innovation—with the chorus singing the words of the "Ode to Joy" by Schiller, the German poet. The Ninth Symphony, a unified work of great dramatic power, translates a wide range of human experience into music. With good reason, many people consider Beethoven the Shakespeare of music.

The Romantic composers of the nineteenth century—Berlioz, Schubert, Mendelssohn, Tchaikovsky and Dvorak—made the symphony colorful and descriptive. The four majestic symphonies of Brahms combine the power of a Beethoven with the warmth and the intimacy of a Romantic.

Among the moderns, Prokofiev, Shostakovich, and Vaughan-Williams have composed outstanding symphonies.

The Concerto

The concerto is one of the large forms of music, in which an individual soloist plays along with the full orchestra. The music written for the soloist is often brilliant and dramatic, giving the performer an opportunity to reveal the variety in expression and in tone color of which his instrument is capable. Some concertos are on the flashy side—vehicles for the virtuoso rather than music for the discerning. But many works in this genre—notably those of Bach, Mozart, Beethoven, Brahms, Prokofiev, and Bartók—represent the best in music.

In the concerto, the theme is often stated first by the orchestra. When the solo instrument enters, the orchestra takes second place, becoming the accompaniment. The alternation of the group statement with the individual statement serves to reveal the music in various settings, an important feature of the concerto form.

The concerto usually has at least one "cadenza" or section in which the orchestra is silent while the soloist plays without accompaniment. In former times the soloist was expected to invent or "improvise" an original passage based on the themes of the concerto. Nowadays, cadenzas are no longer improvised; they are written. Cadenzas, however, still afford the soloist the opportunity to display his capabilities as a musician and his mastery of the instrument.

Ex. 78   Passage for Solo Violin,
from Brahms' Violin Concerto in D Major

Franz Liszt   (in his thirteenth year)

Of the solo instruments used in the concerto form, piano and violin are the most common. You will also hear concertos for cello, flute, clarinet, and even, occasionally, for such instruments as the harp, horn, trumpet, trombone, or bassoon. The French composer, Debussy, has written a composition for saxophone and orchestra. Another Frenchman, Darius Milhaud, has composed a percussion concerto, and the American composer, Paul Creston, a concerto for marimba and orchestra.

Program Music

Program music is not a musical form as is the sonata or the concerto, but rather a certain kind of music that purports to tell a story. This descriptive music may suggest or imitate such sounds as the clash of battle, storms, animal cries, and bird songs.

Telling a story through instrumental music is not modern, as some may suppose. Over two thousand years ago, in ancient Greece, a composer wrote a work describing in music *The Battle of Apollo and Marsyas.* In Shakespeare's time, William Byrd composed a piece for the spinet (one of the ancestors of the piano) depicting *The King's Hunt,* and in the eighteenth century the German composer, Kuhnau, wrote *The Battle of David and Goliath.*

69

More recently, such composers as Berlioz, Liszt, Rimsky-Korsakoff, and Richard Strauss have written many works of program music for symphony orchestra. These compositions are highly descriptive and full of color. Among the most popular are: Berlioz' *Fantastic* Symphony, Rimsky-Korsakoff's *Scheherazade,* and Strauss' *Till Eulenspiegel's Merry Pranks.* Because the listener can imagine a story as he hears the music, many people find such works pleasant and easy to follow.

For the past few decades program music has become less fashionable. Many people find the idea of telling a story through music too obvious, and most composers today have turned away from this type of writing.

So far, the forms we have discussed have been those of instrumental music. Equally interesting are the forms of music built around the human voice.

Vocal Forms

Vocal music, in existence ever since man could sing, has assumed many different shapes. Its earliest forms were, undoubtedly, folk songs (previously discussed), magical music, and religious music.

Almost all religions have a considerable body of chants, hymns, and sacred songs that they use in prayer and in ritual. Roman Catholics have Gregorian chants; Hebrews, their synagogue songs; Protestants, their hymns and their chorales. Most of these sacred songs and chants were created hundred of years ago; many are expressive and beautiful. Hindus Buddhists, Mohammedans, and other religious groups also have their own ritual music.

A great deal of vocal music, both religious and secular, is written for chorus, in which the voices are usually distributed into four sections, having the following vocal ranges:

Ex. 79

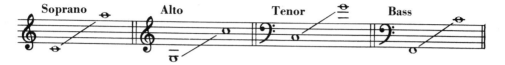

The Mass

In the early days of Christianity, the words of the Mass were intoned or chanted by the priest, with the congregation participating in certain passages. Over a period of several centuries, these chants evolved into set melodies, which later became part of the music of the Roman Catholic service. Pope Gregory the Great (540-604 A.D.) was considered the prime mover in the collecting of this ancient music, and after his death the sacred melodies came to be known as Gregorian Chants.

Later, when harmony and counterpoint began to develop, composers added other parts to the original chants, and by about 1450, the music of the Mass had become very complex, with different voices weaving in and out in intricate fashion.

The Mass reached its high point of beauty about 1550, in the writings of Palestrina and Orlando di Lasso. These works were written *a cappella,* that is, for voices only. Still later, Bach, in the B Minor Mass, and Beethoven, in his *Missa Solemnis,* created two of the monumental religious works of music, in which voices and orchestra were combined.

Chorale, Cantata and Oratorio

When the Protestants separated from the Roman Catholic Church after 1515 and formed another branch of the Christian Church, they altered the traditional forms of religious music. In their desire to have the congregation participate actively in the service, Protestant leaders—Martin Luther especially—developed a new type of sacred song, the "chorale." Whereas Gregorian Chants were difficult to perform, chorales were simple and folklike, encouraging the congregation to join in the singing.

Later on, Johann Sebastian Bach introduced these old German hymn tunes into "cantatas," large compositions for chorus and orchestra, that he wrote for the Lutheran Church. Like other composers, Bach also wrote cantatas on secular subjects, among them the delightful *Peasant* Cantata and the *Coffee* Cantata.

Handel had a brilliant career as an opera composer. He also wrote religious music, excelling in the composing of oratorios. An oratorio is a choral work much longer than a cantata. Some oratorios, containing as many as thirty separate movements, may take two or more hours to play. The plot of an oratorio generally centered on a Biblical character, such as Samson, Moses, or Joshua. Drawing on his operatic experience, Handel chose heroic subjects, and wrote some of the most dramatic choral music of all times.

Most famous of his oratorios is *The Messiah,* which is performed annually during the Christmas season.

Ex. 80   Handel: Hallelujah Chorus, from *The Messiah*

Fresco, Haydn's "The Creation," Vienna Opera House

Other well-known classical oratorios are Handel's *Israel in Egypt,* Haydn's *The Creation,* and Mendelssohn's *Elijah.*

In recent years composers have written very successful choral works on a variety of subjects. Among the most interesting of these are *King David* and *Joan of Arc at the Stake* by Arthur Honegger, the *Symphony of Psalms* by Stravinsky, *Belshazzar's Feast* by William Walton, and *Alexander Nevsky* by Prokofiev.

The Madrigal

Although many choral compositions are religious, an equal number, perhaps, deals with love, springtime, dancing, and other worldly subjects.

About four hundred years ago, choral music of this worldly character reached its flower in the "madrigal." The madrigal, a secular composition for small chorus, is often written in complex counterpoint with playful, tricky rhythms. In the days of Queen Elizabeth, four or five

people would gather around a table in someone's home and spend an evening singing madrigals for pleasure. England made its finest contribution to music through the madrigals of Thomas Morley, William Byrd, Thomas Weelkes, and other Elizabethan composers.

Claudio Monteverdi was a great Italian madrigal composer of the sixteenth and seventeenth centuries. Claude Le Jeune and Orlando di Lasso wrote charming French madrigals.

Lieder and the Song Cycle

An important type of vocal music that appeared at the beginning of the nineteenth century is the song for solo voice with piano accompaniment. It is sometimes called the "art song," to distinguish it from the folk or popular song. The main quality of an art song is not only its tunefulness, but also its success in conveying subtle emotions. Composers frequently use great poems for their art songs, and the composer's task is to fit the music to the intimate and delicate shades of meaning in the words.

Many of the subtle shadings in the art song are suggested by the piano accompaniment—often as important in this form of music as is the vocal part itself.

The Germans call art songs *Lieder*. German composers, particularly Schubert, Schumann, Brahms, and Wolf, excelled in this sort of composition. The outstanding writers of art songs in France have been Debussy, Gabriel Fauré, and Francis Poulenc.

74

Schubert's Birthplace

Moussorgsky wrote many Russian songs of a realistic, satirical, and dramatic character, among them, the "Songs and Dances of Death." Charles Ives' songs, notably "Charlie Rutlage" and "General William Booth Enters Heaven," assert the down-to-earth qualities of the American people.

A group of songs related in mood or with a continuous story is called a "song cycle." One of the most beautiful of these is Schubert's *Die Schöne Müllerin, The Miller's Beautiful Daughter.*

Ex. 81 Schubert: The Miller's Beautiful Daughter

I — heard a cool brook mur - mur-ing and bub-bling down the hill.

4

Opera and Musical Theater

Verdi

Opera is a play in which the words are sung instead of spoken. More than that, it is a combination of the arts—music (singing and orchestral playing), drama, poetry, painting, the dance, and in some instances architecture. It is difficult to fuse all these elements into a single art form, but when this is done successfully, the results are magnificent.

Why is it that some people who like musical theater do not care for opera and consider it absurd? The main reason, I believe, is that in America, until recently, operas have usually been sung in foreign languages, seldom in English. In Norway, operas are given in Norwegian; in Holland, they are sung in Dutch. It seems obvious that people who pay to see a show—and opera is a kind of show—want to understand what the actors are saying or singing. Opera is a story in music. When a listener cannot follow the plot of a story, he is apt to find the performance boring, no matter how beautiful the music may be. No wonder then that some people do not care for opera!

What are the qualities of a good opera? Basically, opera needs an interesting story, a colorful setting, and distinctive characters. We cannot help being attracted by *Don Giovanni,* deeply interested in the fate of *Boris Godunov,* or intrigued by *Carmen.* There is tense drama in Verdi's *Otello,* in Puccini's *Tosca,* and in Berg's *Wozzeck.* The setting of Catfish Row lends color to *Porgy and Bess;* the Latin Quarter street scene is one of the highlights of Puccini's *La Bohème.*

Story alone has never made a great opera. The heart of an opera is its music, which must be moving, expressive, and, above all, dramatic. The finest composers of operas have been creative musicians who were also men of the theater.

76

Paris Opera House

Aria, Recitative, and Ensemble

Every opera composer knows that one of the important ingredients of successful opera is the "aria." Aria is the Italian word for "air," or song, but a song of a special kind.

A good aria must meet three requirements. First, it must have a fresh, distinctive melody. Secondly, it should express the personality of the operatic character who sings it. A light, tuneful aria such as "La Donna è Mobile" ("Woman Is Changeable") reveals the flippant nature of the Duke in Verdi's *Rigoletto.*

Ex. 82 Verdi: Woman is Changeable, from *Rigoletto*

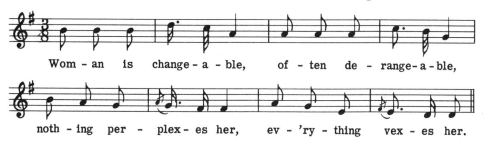

The melody of "It Ain't Necessarily So," from Gershwin's *Porgy and Bess*, twists, slides, and curves. It portrays—even without the words—the slippery, two-faced character of Sportin' Life.

The third requirement of a good aria is that the various colors of the voice and the techniques of singing be used to express ideas or emotions.

Besides the arias, there are many passages in opera where two or more characters sing together—duets, trios, quartets, etc. These "ensembles," as they are called, are often highly dramatic.

A good example of ensemble is the scene in *Porgy and Bess* where a mother sings a lullaby ("Summertime") to her child. At the same time, a group of men shoot dice and sing about the game in jazz rhythms. The contrast between the two melodies makes for effective theater and adds much to the appeal of the opera.

Another device used in opera is "recitative." The word means "talking-in-music," or intoning on various pitch levels in a free rhythm. The musical effect of recitative is secondary. Its main purpose is to tell the audience certain facts about the plot of the opera or its characters. Dramatic action slows down when a long aria is sung merely to tell where someone lives, or that a door key has been lost. Recitative communicates the facts with dispatch. In his opera *La Bohème*, Puccini has Mimi and Rodolfo communicate just such facts to the audience in a delicate, poetic recitative. The effect is enchanting.

Though the emphasis in most operas is on the voices, the orchestra, too, is essential. It acts as background for the singers and helps to create the desired mood. In the crowd scene in the last act of Bizet's *Carmen,* brilliant orchestration establishes a gay and festive air. The orchestra plays throughout the opera—ballet scenes, overtures, interludes. At moments when the characters on stage are silent, the orchestral music may interpret their moods and emotions. When the characters leave the stage, the music may establish the mood of the scene to follow.

There are many different kinds of operas, from the sparkling comedies of Mozart, *The Marriage of Figaro* and *Così fan tutte (Women Are*

Scene from "Porgy and Bess"

Like That), to Richard Wagner's "music dramas," *Lohengrin* and *The Valkyrie*. Puccini wrote the romantic and tuneful *La Bohème* and *Madame Butterfly*. Verdi's *Aïda* is one of the most famous "grand operas," complete with splendid arias, stately choruses, elaborate settings, and pageantry.

Opera in English

America's interest in opera has increased, in recent years, with the many opportunities for hearing the classical operas sung in English. Television productions have been especially effective in awakening an interest in opera among the many people who have never been inside an opera house.

Even more significant than the performance of the translated opera is the appearance of operas originally written in English. Gershwin's *Porgy and Bess,* composed in 1935, was the first truly successful American opera. Strangely enough, it was written for the theater and known as "musical drama." At that time, people were wary of the word "opera," and it was only by masquerading under another name that *Porgy* could be produced.

Each Christmas for the past few years, another opera written in English, Menotti's *Amahl and the Night Visitors,* has gone into millions of American homes by way of the television screen and has given pleasure to countless viewers.

Among other American operas, the most successful have been Marc Blitzstein's *The Cradle Will Rock,* Carlyle Floyd's *Susanna,* Gian-Carlo Menotti's *The Medium* and *The Consul,* Douglas Moore's *Ballad of Baby Doe,* and Kurt Weill's *Down in the Valley.* When the words of an opera are understood, the audience can fully participate in the dramatic action. For this reason, opera is becoming a popular form of American theater.

Musical Comedy

Turning from opera to musical comedy, we enter a different world. Musical values and serious expression are uppermost in opera, but in musical comedy the main objective is entertainment. And the entertainment that musical comedy offers is often dazzling.

The theater has always welcomed light music—the music of Gilbert and Sullivan, Offenbach, Johann Strauss, vaudeville tunes. But it is only in the American musical comedy that popular musical theater has achieved a speed and a vitality that makes it one of the most sought-after forms of entertainment.

Good musical comedies, or musical plays, as some of them are recently described, gives the audience a dash of everything, switching rapidly from tuneful songs to dramatic scenes, from exuberant dances to hilarious comedy situations, from lush choral numbers to brassy music in the orchestra. Everything moves in a quick, modern stage tempo, and not a moment is left unaccounted for. No one has the chance to tire of one scene before the curtain rises on another carefully contrasted scene. Add the brilliant settings, the pretty chorus girls, the splashy costumes, and it is easy to see why the musical show has such tremendous appeal for the average theatergoer.

80

Jazz is an important element of many, but not all, musicals. In some shows, *Brigadoon* by Lerner and Loewe or *The King and I* by Rodgers and Hammerstein, for example, the tunes lean toward the romantic. But whether the songs are bouncy or lyrical, the composer must "plug" them; that is, he must make sure that two or three of the best numbers in the show are repeated often enough to make the audience remember them afterwards.

One of the subtle ingredients of a good musical is the special atmosphere it creates—the illusion of being in a particular time and place, a place that never existed, perhaps, except in the sights and sounds of the theater. The Siam of *The King and I* is certainly not the true, historical Siam. Nor was there ever a Southland like the magical one in Harburg and Lane's *Finian's Rainbow*. Yet when you visit these fictional places and meet the fictional people in them, you come away with the feeling that they really do exist. The musical theater seems to be a place of magic.

The plots of musicals are often frothy, sometimes even absurd. In recent years, however, there has been a trend toward more literate, dramatic stories. Rodgers and Hammerstein were innovators in this field, with *Carousel,* based on Ferenc Molnar's play, *Liliom.* Kurt Weill and

Maxwell Anderson derived the story of *Lost in the Stars* from the novel, *Cry, the Beloved Country,* by Alan Paton. Lerner and Loewe scored one of the great theatrical successes of our time when they turned Bernard Shaw's *Pygmalion* into the musical, *My Fair Lady.*

When the script and the score of a Broadway musical are first-rate, as in Harburg and Lane's *Finian's Rainbow,* or in Loesser, Burrows, and Swerling's *Guys and Dolls,* the productions are no longer mere entertainment; they have become a superb form of musical theater.

A most interesting development is the growing influence of opera and musical comedy upon each other. *The Threepenny Opera,* in a class by itself, is based on John Gay's witty eighteenth-century satire, *The Beggar's Opera.* Kurt Weill, in his deliberately harsh yet haunting music, and Berthold Brecht, in his ironic text, created a bitter indictment of the folly and hypocrisy of our times.

Sometimes it is difficult to decide whether a show, such as *The Threepenny Opera* or Leonard Bernstein and Arthur Laurents' *West Side Story,* is a musical or an opera. Perhaps, in the future, a new form will emerge in which the elements of both musical comedy and opera will be combined.

Vienna Opera House

Operetta

Though its death was predicted a number of years ago, operetta refuses to die. It lives on to satisfy the sentimental streak inherent in many of us.

Operetta has elements of both opera and musical comedy. Its plot often deals with a romantic, imaginary kingdom; the dialogue is more genteel than that in a musical comedy; the music is more waltz-like than "jazzy." Many operettas, Johann Strauss' *Die Fledermaus (The Bat)* and Offenbach's *La Périchole,* have touches of operatic style, including recitative, ensembles, and florid writing for the voice.

Although sentiment is supposed to be unfashionable in this "hard-boiled" age, Jerome Kern and Oscar Hammerstein's *Show Boat,* a frankly sentimental operetta, has proved to be the perennial favorite of American theatergoers.

Film Music

A relatively new field for the theater composer is film music. Hollywood producers have a much-overworked maxim: the best film score is the one least noticed by the audience. The absurdity of this notion is proved by the success of the motion pictures that do have outstanding scores—films such as *Alexander Nevsky,* with music by Prokofiev; *Hamlet,* with a score by William Walton; *A Streetcar Named Desire,* scored by Alex North.

Film music should, of course, be an organic part of the film, not an unrelated ornament. When a gifted composer has created a fine film score, audiences cannot help being aware of it, for it adds to their pleasure.

As it does for the theater, good music enhances the film—it can create mood, accent a dramatic scene, or reveal the inner emotions of a character. In addition, music acts as a bridge for scene changes and camera "dissolves" that are needed to produce a smooth effect. A fine score contributes to the unity, power, and poetic quality of a motion picture.

Ballet Music

Ballet music is often characterized by vigorous, distinctive rhythms and colorful orchestration. Since dance is movement, many types and variations of rhythm are called for in the ballet.

In classical ballet, the formal patterning of the dance movement required orderly, regular rhythms in the music. The romantic charm of Tchaikovsky's scores for *Swan Lake* and *The Nutcracker* has made them favorites in ballet repertoire.

Modern dance, in its exploration of new types of movement, demanded new concepts in the composing of music for the ballet. Choreographers and producers, such as Diaghilev, Balanchine, and Martha Graham, have stimulated the writing of modern ballet music in France and in the United States.

The greatest of recent ballet composers is Stravinsky, who wrote *The Fire Bird, Petroushka,* and *The Rite of Spring.* Ravel's *Daphnis and Chloë,* Copland's *Appalachian Spring,* and Prokofiev's *Romeo and Juliet* are other distinguished works written for the modern ballet.

5

The Orchestra and Its Instruments

The symphony orchestra, with its richness, precision, and beauty of tone, is a proud artistic achievement of western civilization. Symphonic organizations have existed for centuries, but never before has their music attained such brilliance and expressive power as is heard in our time. Depending upon the music performed, the orchestral concert can be a feast for the ear, a challenge to the mind, or an experience for the emotions. Learning how to listen to a symphony orchestra is an art each individual must cultivate for himself.

The instruments of the orchestra may be classified as stringed instruments, wood winds, brasses, and percussion instruments.

The Conductor

Sometimes, musicians in the orchestra question the importance of the conductor's role. This attitude may at times be justified, but such occasions are rare. Orchestras would quickly dispense with conductors if it were feasible. The performance would collapse, however, without the leadership of the man who waves the stick.

The movements of the conductor's arms are only a small part of his task. Far more important than the movements of his baton are the workings of his mind. A conductor is responsible for understanding the musical score and for the precise balance of sound of, perhaps, one hundred instruments playing at the same time.

But that is not all the conductor does. He instructs each performer, indicating the particular shading of a phrase and the quality and the volume of tone each instrument must produce to blend with the other sounds. A conductor must not only be a fine musician; he must be a showman and a psychologist as well. He must evoke the best qualities of each player, in order to achieve the utmost precision and refinement of the conductor's instrument—the symphony orchestra.

Stringed Instruments Played with Bows

Stringed instruments are played by drawing a bow of horsehair over a gut or metal string. Rubbing a bow across the tightly stretched string causes it to vibrate, and thus helps to create the sound.

Because strings, only, do not produce much tone, they are attached to a hollow, wooden body. This body vibrates along with the strings, augmenting the sound of the instrument.

The string section of the orchestra consists of violins, violas, cellos, and double basses.

The Violin

The violin is the smallest member of the string family. Its four strings are held away from the wooden body by a small bridge. Usually only one string of the violin is played at a time. A violinist can, however, sound two strings at once to produce two notes, an effect called "double stopping." More rarely, three or even four strings may be played with one stroke of the bow. By plucking the strings with his fingers, the violinist can make a sharp, short sound, called "pizzicato." When a "mute" is attached to the strings, the violin has a soft, velvety tone.

The symphony orchestra may use as many as thirty-two violins, which are divided into two groups: First Violins and Second Violins. A fine violin section can play with varied shadings, warmth, and sweetness. Violins form the backbone of the orchestra and play a more important role in orchestral music than does any other single group of instruments.

Violin

Ex. 83   Mendelssohn: Violin Concerto in E Minor

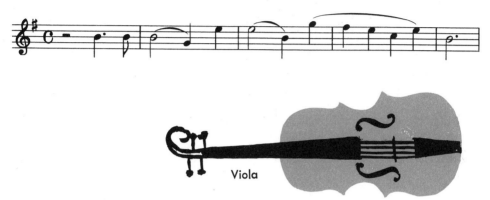

Viola

The Viola

The viola may be described as an outsized violin. It is about a fifth larger in size and five tones deeper in pitch than the violin, and it is slightly rougher in sound. At one time, orchestral music written for the viola part was quite elementary and dull, consisting mainly of accompanying tones and afterbeats.

More recently, composers have discovered that, although the viola does not have the clear, ringing tone of the violin, it does have a distinctive character of its own. Music of a vigorous or throaty quality is now often given to the viola. As a result, viola players no longer consider themselves second-class members of the orchestra.

Ex. 84   Brahms: Symphony No. 3

Cello

The Cello

A French political leader used to deliver speeches in such a rich, throbbing voice that he was nicknamed "the cello." The cello, or violoncello, to give it a formal name, is one of the great "singers" of the orchestra.

The cellist sits with his instrument held between the knees. The instrument has long strings and is played with a rather large bow. A cello can produce deep, mellow tones as well as high, intense ones. Its sound is penetrating and vibrant, and in the upper range, the tone of the cello can cut through the sound of the entire orchestra.

Beethoven, Wagner, Tchaikovsky, and many other composers gave some of their warmest melodies to the cello.

Ex. 85   Saint-Saëns: The Swan, from *Carnival of Animals*

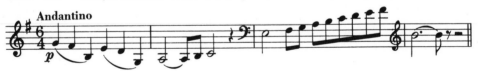

The Double Bass

When an orchestra travels from one concert hall to another, the man with a problem may well be the double bass player, who must, at times, carry his own giant instrument. Except for the percussionist, he is the only performer who plays standing up.

Double Bass

The double bass usually plays the lowest tones in the orchestra. A good bass section gives support to the other instruments; its tone is the foundation of the orchestral sound.

A bass player must possess strong hands to press the heavy strings down against the wood, and he also must have the skill to make the wide finger stretches that the size of his instrument demands. The double bass is played in the jazz band, as well as in the symphony orchestra. In the jazz band, the bass is most frequently played pizzicato in a rhythmic way. A good bass player must have what jazz men call "a solid beat."

Ex. 86 Prokofiev: *Lieutenant Kijé* Suite

Wood-Wind Instruments

The sound of wood-wind instruments is produced by air passing through a pipe. One end of the pipe has a mouthpiece, and, as in all wood winds except the flute and the piccolo, the mouthpiece is fitted with a small strip of cane called a "reed." Air blown across the reed causes it to vibrate, thus producing the special "reedy" tone.

Every wood wind has holes that are bored along the side of the pipe. By opening or closing the holes, the player can produce various notes within the range of his instrument. When a hole is opened, the air space in the pipe is shortened. The shorter the air space of the pipe, the higher the tone; the longer the air space, the deeper the tone.

At one time, all wood-wind instruments were made of wood—hence the name, wood wind. Today, one of the loveliest of all, the flute, is made of metal, most often silver. It still, however, retains its membership in the wood-wind family. Each variety of instrument in this family has its unique timbre that can be clearly recognized in the orchestral sound. Wood winds are individualists.

The Flute

The flute is the high soprano voice of the wood winds. Its bright, clear tone often rises far above all the other sounds.

Ex. 87 Tchaikovsky: Dance of the Reed Pipes, from the *Nutcracker* Suite

No instrument can equal the flute for the playing of delicate, pure, poetic melodies. With its amazing powers to perform fast, brilliant passages, the flute can produce so many notes in such a short time that it suggests a burst of fireworks. It can also play soft, tender, low notes, as Debussy proved in *The Afternoon of a Faun.* (See "Debussy" in Chapter 7, under Great Modern Composers.)

Piccolo

The Piccolo

A small edition of the flute is the piccolo, the "little" flute. Its brilliant tone is pitched an octave higher than that of the flute. Clear and piercing, the piccolo can even be heard when the entire orchestra is playing fortissimo. In many of Sousa's marches, the high trill of the piccolo sings out clearly over the pounding brasses.

Oboe

The Oboe

Almost all instruments vary in pitch under different weather conditions; but the pitch of the oboe is the most constant of all. That is why the members of the orchestra tune their instruments to the oboe's "A." If you listen carefully as an orchestra tunes up, one of the first notes you may hear is that of the oboist, giving the pitch.

The sound of the oboe is sweet and intense, suitable for tender melodies and also for folklike tunes. It is a double-reed instrument, and is played by blowing air between two thin pieces of reed, which are tightly clamped together in the mouthpiece, causing them to vibrate. Tchaikovsky used the oboe for a melodic solo in his Fourth Symphony.

Ex. 88 Tchaikovsky: Symphony No. 4

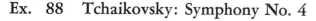

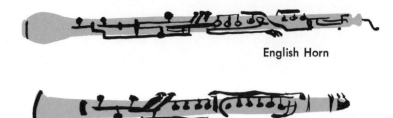

English Horn

Clarinet

The English Horn

A close relative of the oboe, with a rather illogical name, is known as the English horn. Someone has pointed out that the English horn is neither English nor a horn. The instrument is a larger, deep-toned oboe with a bulblike end. Its rich, full tone differs from that of the oboe— the tone quality of the English horn is haunting and often rather sad. Once you have heard Dvorak's *New World* Symphony, you will never forget the sound of the English horn playing the famous "Going Home" melody.

Ex. 89 Dvorak: Symphony No. 5, *From the New World*

The Clarinet

The clarinet, the greatest "mixer" of all the wood winds, appears in the symphony orchestra, the marching band, and the jazz band. Some concert bands have as many as thirty clarinets.

Perhaps the reason the clarinet is so widely used lies in the variety of tone qualities it can produce. In its middle range, the sound of the clarinet is full and sweet. In the low range, it is dark and threatening. Do you recall the ominous low tones of the Cat theme in *Peter and the Wolf?*

Ex. 90   Prokofiev: *Peter and the Wolf*

p

The highest notes, often favored by jazz clarinetists, are piercing and vibrant. A good player of the "licorice stick," the jazz man's name for the clarinet, can really "send" an audience.

Clarinets are made in large and in small sizes, in addition to the regular size, which is two feet long. Because the little, or E flat, clarinet, has an especially shrill high register, composers have often employed it for comic or grotesque effects, as in Strauss' *Till Eulenspiegel's Merry Pranks.*

The Bass Clarinet is a large, deep-toned instrument with an upturned bell. Tchaikovsky loved its velvety, creamy tone, and used it effectively in the *Nutcracker* Suite.

The Bassoon

Occasionally, the bassoon is described as the "clown of the orchestra," although its music is frequently sober, pensive, or even poetic. The instrument is a wooden tube, nine feet long, doubled back upon itself to make for easier holding. The bell of the bassoon points upward when played.

The lowest sounds of the wood winds are usually produced by the bassoon. It is played in the weird, perky tune of the *Sorcerer's Apprentice.*

Ex. 91   Dukas: *Sorcerer's Apprentice*

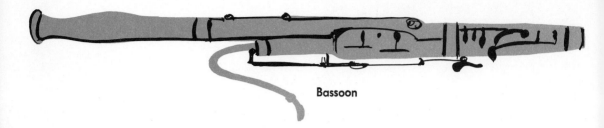

Bassoon

An instrument that often does play the clown is the Contrabassoon. With eighteen feet of tubing, its sound lies an octave lower than that of the bassoon.

For comic effects, the contrabassoon grunts and moans as no other instrument can. Ravel used this instrument to portray the Beast in the movement Beauty and the Beast from his *Mother Goose* Suite.

Brass Instruments

Because of their power, brass instruments are sometimes thought of as the "heavy artillery" of the orchestra. These instruments, however, can also be played softly and with delicate shading. Since this requires great control of the lips and the breath, brass instruments are difficult to play.

The French Horn

The ancestor of this instrument was a hunting horn. With its broad, flaring bell and its coiled brass tubing, often as long as eighteen feet, the French horn makes a striking picture. Modern French horns usually have three valves. When a valve is pressed, the length of the tubing is altered. This helps the player to produce various tones.

Four or more horns are generally used in the symphony orchestra. When they harmonize, they produce a wonderfully warm, resonant tone. In loud passages, the horns are crackling and powerful. In soft

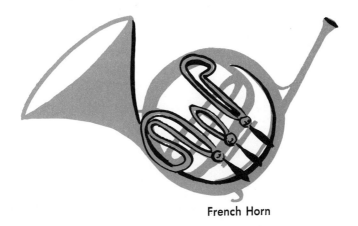

French Horn

passages, they have a mellow, dreamlike quality. Tchaikovsky wrote beautifully for the solo horn in the slow movement of his Fifth Symphony.

Ex. 92   Tchaikovsky: Symphony No. 5

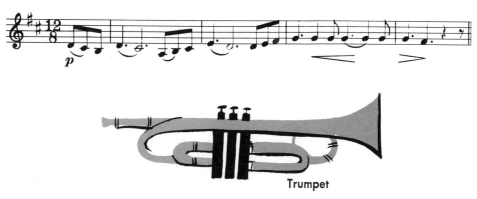

Trumpet

The Trumpet

Because its tone is vigorous and penetrating, it is easy to recognize the trumpet. This instrument owes much to its ancestor, the bugle, which was used to signal the charge on the battlefield. Like the French horn, the trumpet has three valves.

Ex. 93   Stravinsky: *Petroushka*

The clear, ringing tone of the trumpet is thrilling when it sounds forth at the height of a great orchestral climax. Equally magical is its softer tone, which can be produced with or without a mute. The brassy, nasal sounds of muted trumpets are favored in dance music and in jazz.

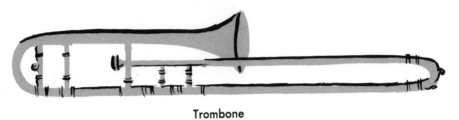

Trombone

The Trombone

Many instruments are interesting to see as they are being played. One of the best instruments to watch is the trombone, whose pitch is varied by a slide. The player raises or lowers the pitch by moving the slide in or out. In circus or jazz band, the trombonist often uses the comic, smearing effect known as "glissando."

In symphonic music, the trombone is often used for powerful, majestic, or solemn passages. In the jazz band, it may be played with a throaty, wobbling tone, called "vibrato," in imitation of the voice of a blues singer. The trombone in the military band adds much to the challenging sound of the music. Richard Wagner gave the melody in the *Tannhäuser* Overture to the trombone.

Ex. 94   Wagner: *Tannhäuser* Overture

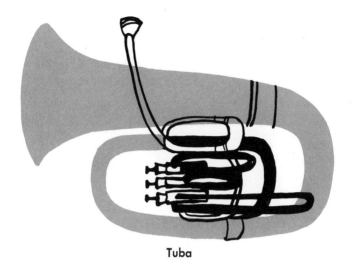

Tuba

The Tuba

Ever since George Kleinsinger wrote *Tubby the Tuba,* we know that every tuba player has a soul. Compelled to play mostly "oom-pahs," the tuba is the largest and the deepest-toned of the brass instruments. It has a wide bell, long winding tubing, and valves. If you watch a tuba player closely, you will notice that he takes in great draughts of air in order to make his giant instrument sound. The tuba is essential in the brass band, where its strong, deep sounds combine with those of the bass drum to set the rhythm of the march. It also serves to strengthen the lowest tones of the orchestra.

Ex. 95   Wagner: Overture to *The Mastersingers of Nuremberg*

Percussion Instruments

Percussion instruments are those that are struck, clapped together, or shaken to make them sound. For this reason some people think they are easy to play, and that a drummer is a second-rate musician who just bangs away at his "kitchenware." A fine percussionist, like other musicians, needs long training, a keen sense of rhythm, and a delicate ear.

The Timpani

The most important percussion instruments are the drums; and in the drum section, the aristocrats are the kettledrums, or timpani. These drums are large copper bowls with parchment stretched tightly over the rims. Timpani are the only drums that are tuned to definite pitches. Often the player must change the pitch of his timpani in the middle of a composition. It requires a fine ear to do this while the whole orchestra is playing fortissimo.

The Bass Drum

The bass drum is carried in every parade. It also helps to build up a climax in the symphony orchestra. In the jazz band, the drummer, who usually plays two or three instruments at once, uses a foot pedal with which he taps the big drum.

The Snare Drum

The snare drum produces a brittle, crackling sound. It is a small double-headed drum with parchment covering the two heads, and strings, or "snares," stretched across the bottom of the instrument. In the symphony orchestra the snare drum player normally uses two wooden sticks. A drummer needs considerable skill to produce the various rolls and rhythmic accents written for this instrument. In the jazz band, the drummer often plays the snare drum with two wire brushes that give the soft rhythmic beat so important in dance music.

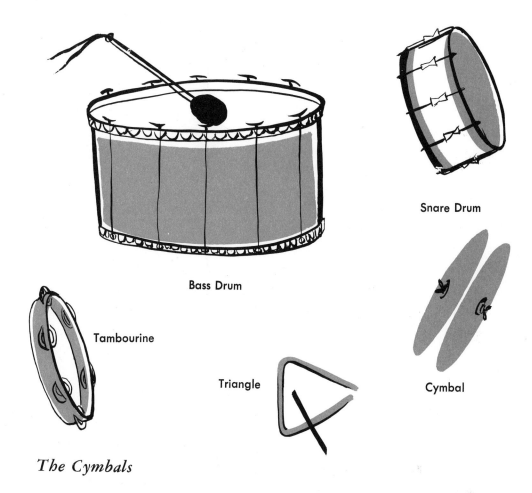

Bass Drum

Snare Drum

Tambourine

Triangle

Cymbal

The Cymbals

At times the jazz drummer shifts his wire brushes over to a cymbal, a wide brass plate supported by a stand. The rhythmic "swoosh, swoosh" sound of this instrument is exciting.

For orchestral playing, cymbals usually come in pairs and are most often clashed together to make a glorious noise. When the cymbals are clashed, the player may turn them outward towards the audience, so that the continuing vibrations may be heard.

Other Percussion Instruments

Included among the percussion instruments is the Tambourine, which is a circular "head" covered with parchment. Metallic discs, or jingles, surround the rim. The instrument is shaken or struck.

The Triangle is a small metal bar bent into the shape from which it takes its name. When struck with a small beater, it produces a bright, clear sound.

The Castanets, the Cowbell, and the Wood Block are also percussion instruments and are mainly used in compositions of a theatrical or descriptive character.

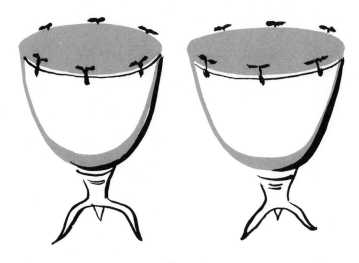

Timpani

The Xylophone is made of parallel pieces of hardwood, cut in graduated sizes to give different pitches, and mounted on a frame. It may have resonators attached to the bars for enhancing the sound. Played with hard mallets, the xylophone produces dry, brittle tones.

Resembling the xylophone, the Glockenspiel, or "bells," is made of short metal bars, and is played with two mallets, hard or soft. The tone is glittering and clear.

Tubular Chimes consist of long, hollow, metal pipes suspended on a frame. The sound approximates the full, vibrant tone of church bells.

The Celeste looks like a small upright piano, but has a keyboard of only four octaves instead of the seven octaves plus of the piano. Its hammers strike metal bars which are placed over hollow, wooden boxes. The tone is poetic, bell-like, even heavenly, "celestial"—hence the name, celeste.

More Instruments

Until about fifty years ago, the instruments so far described, plus the harp, were the only instruments considered proper in the symphony orchestra. In recent years, composers have added new sounds to the traditional ones. Among the instruments occasionally used in modern scores are the piano, the saxophone, the organ, and the guitar.

Piano

The Piano

The piano is a combination string-and-percussion instrument. Its eighty-eight keys are attached to hammers, which produce sound by striking the metal strings. To examine the mechanism of a piano, open the top and look inside as you strike a note on the keyboard. You will then see something like this:

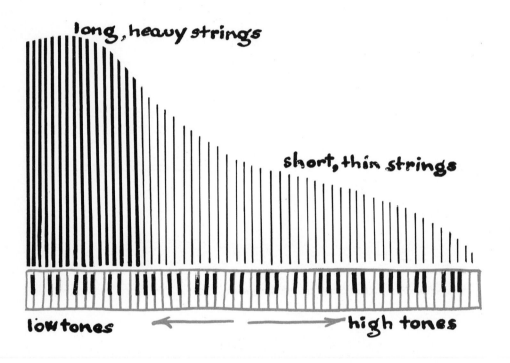

Although the piano has an important role in modern orchestral music, it is mainly used as a solo instrument. It is, perhaps, the one instrument on which music of almost any kind—piano music; songs, jazz, opera, and theater music; symphonies—can be played. Playing the piano is probably the best way to acquire a knowledge of the different types and styles of music. Many of the world's great composers have been pianists.

The Harp

The harp is one of the oldest stringed instruments known to man. Its tone is delicate and poetic. There is nothing quite so ethereal as the glissando—an effect created when the harpist runs his fingers lightly over the strings.

The harp consists of forty-seven strings set in a triangular frame. Its chief uses in the orchestra are to give velvety richness to the general sound and to serve as a background for solos played by other instruments. Ravel featured the harp as a solo instrument in his Introduction and Allegro.

The Saxophone

The saxophone, named after its inventor, Adolph Sax, is a strange instrument—part wood wind and part brass. At first, it was employed

Saxophone

mostly in military bands where it still serves a useful purpose. More recently it has been added to the jazz band. Negro jazz men used to play the saxophone as they played the trombone—with a strong vibrato, in imitation of the blues singer. Since this quality was well suited to express the jazz musicians' feelings, the saxophone became a permanent part of the jazz band.

In more recent years composers such as Gershwin, Ravel, and Villa-Lobos have occasionally used it in the symphony orchestra.

The Organ

In addition to its ancient role in the history of music, the organ has two other claims to distinction—it can produce the widest range of pitch and the greatest volume of tone of any single instrument.

Throughout history, the organ has been closely associated with church music. Most of the great compositions written for the organ were created by famous musicians, notably Bach, among others who wrote for the church. Nothing is quite so impressive as a fine organ sounding forth in a great church or a cathedral.

Organ

The tone of the organ is produced by air passing through a large number of pipes of various sizes. The organ has at least two manuals (keyboards) and a set of foot pedals on which bass notes are usually played. In addition, there are a great many "stops"—knobs—which when pulled out produce various mixtures of tone. All these features contribute to the variety and the power of sounds made by the organ.

Because of the expense involved in building a pipe organ, inventors have tried to duplicate its sound by electronic means. Now, many small organs are being widely used in radio and television stations to provide background music for programs.

The Guitar

Although extensively used today as an accompaniment for folk songs, the guitar in its original form was not a folk instrument. A thousand years ago, it was played by highly trained musicians in Persia. In the Middle Ages, the Moors brought the guitar with them to Spain. Today, Spanish guitarists are highly skilled professionals with a superb command of the delicate instrument.

The guitar has six strings that are plucked with the thumb and fingers, or with a pick. Because it produces little sound, the guitar is most often heard in small jazz bands or in theater orchestras. Some guitars have electrical attachments to amplify the sound of the instrument.

Guitar

Ludwig van Beethoven

6

Our Musical Heritage

A contrast between Classical and Romantic composers is often noted. The Classical composer was mainly concerned with the structure, the proportions, and the formal design of his music. His compositions were objective, not reflections of his passions or moods. Sometimes it is difficult to distinguish the work of one Classical composer from that of his contemporaries—the music of Mozart and of Haydn often sounds alike; the compositions of Bach and of Handel have much in common.

To the Romantic composer, emotion, originality, and autobiographical qualities were all-important. The Romanticist was more concerned with color, drama, and sensory values than with form. Romantic compositions may be loosely constructed, but rich in atmospheric qualities and moods. Emotional communication was of the essence of this music, the design or form of the music of secondary importance.

One should be careful, however, not to draw too rigid a line between the Classicists and the Romanticists. Composers who lived between the years 1750 and 1820 are usually considered Classicists, and those who lived between 1820 and 1890 are thought of as Romanticists.

But many so-called Classicists, including Bach, Mozart, and especially Beethoven, often display the subjectivity, the moods, and the coloristic traits usually thought of as Romantic.

Conversely, many dyed-in-the-wool Romanticists, notably Mendelssohn, Chopin, and Brahms, strove for clear outlines, logical construction, and beauty of form with as much zeal as any Classicist. Actually, almost every composer possesses some attributes of the Classical and some of the Romantic in his make-up.

Great Composers of the Past

Much has been written about the lives and the music of the great composers whose music has endured. On the following pages, you will find biographical sketches of some of the men who contributed to the growth of music as an art. For further reading, see the bibliography in Chapter 11.

Giovanni Pierluigi da Palestrina (1525?-1594), born near Rome, Italy, is the most famous of the composers who wrote for the Catholic Church. Unlike other masters of his time who composed secular as well as sacred music, he devoted himself to the writing of unaccompanied, polyphonic church music. His compositions, which include 102 Masses, 450 motets, and other sacred works, were distinguished for their flowing melodies, serene beauty, and purity of style. In an age when many composers were expressing the Renaissance passion for living even in the music they wrote for the Church, Palestrina glorified the mystical

Giovanni Pierluigi da Palestrina

side of religion. The *Missa Papae Marcelli* and his settings for *The Song of Solomon* are representative of his works. The Church recognized him as its leading composer. In his time and afterwards, Palestrina was called the "Prince of Music."

Orlando di Lasso

Orlando di Lasso (1532?-1594) was a brilliant composer of the Renaissance. Though most of his music was written for chorus, he was able to achieve amazing variety in his work—from earthy street songs and love songs to the most exalted religious music. Lasso was so widely sought after that kings vied with each other for the privilege of having him write for their courts. He composed Masses for the Pope in Rome, and madrigals for the King of France and for noblemen in Flanders and Germany. One of the few true internationalists in musical history,

110

Lasso captured in his music the spirit of each of the various countries in which he lived.

Ex. 96   Orlando di Lasso: Chanson (Transposed)

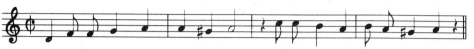

When my old man comes home at night,   All he knows is how to beat me.

Thomas Morley (1557-1603?), great English composer of Shakespeare's day, expressed in his madrigals the delights of youth, love, and springtime in refreshing dance rhythms. Like other Elizabethan composers, he had a complete command of the art of setting English poetry to music. Morley also wrote many pieces for the virginal—a delicate-sounding keyboard instrument that was one of the ancestors of the piano. Some of his music was dedicated to Queen Elizabeth. Among his compositions are "Now Is the Month of Maying," "It Was a Lover and His Lass," and "Oh, Mistress Mine."

Ex. 97   Morley: Now Is the Month of Maying

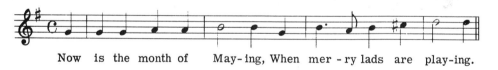

Now   is   the   month of   May-ing, When mer - ry lads are play-ing.

Claudio Monteverdi (1567-1643) was a pioneer in music. At a time when most composers created in contrapuntal style, Monteverdi wrote music for the solo voice with an instrumental accompaniment of chords. This style is, of course, commonplace today, but around 1600 it was revolutionary. After writing many beautiful Italian madrigals, the composer turned to the then new form, opera, and created the first great music dramas in history.

Claudio Monteverdi

Monteverdi's finest works include the operas, *Orfeo* and *The Coronation of Poppea*. His music was so passionate and so tender that, at some performances of his operas, the entire audience, it was said, burst into tears.

Ex. 98   Monteverdi: *Orfeo*

Come, love-ly girls leave the moun-tains, come ___ and leave the foun-tains.

Henry Purcell (1658-1695). From the days of Queen Elizabeth to the present time, no English composer has won more laurels than Henry Purcell. His music is dramatic—with sharp dissonances, abrupt changes in dynamics, and vivid descriptive passages that reflect his interest in the theater. He wrote many songs, choral works, sonatas, and fantasies for various instruments, besides composing music for over fifty stage productions, including two of Shakespeare's plays.

Purcell's masterpiece was *Dido and Aeneas,* possibly the finest opera created by an English composer, and written, oddly enough, for a girls' school. The work is distinguished for its dramatic power and its skillful marriage of words and music. One of the opera's most beautiful arias is the deeply moving lament of Dido, "When I Am Laid in Earth."

Henry Purcell

Johann Sebastian Bach

Johann Sebastian Bach (1685-1760), during his lifetime, was known as a superb performer on the organ. Not until about a hundred years after his death was he recognized as a great composer. Admiration for his work continues to grow, and today Bach is considered one of the supreme masters of music.

Bach was a great family man—he had twenty-one children. Despite family cares, he found time to write an incredible amount of music, including hundreds of religious cantatas, as many works for the clavichord or harpsichord, and a vast number of compositions for organ, violin, cello, flute, and other solo instruments, as well as for orchestra. Bach's counterpoint is magnificent, and his sense of form remains unsurpassed to this day. His music is far more highly honored now than it was when the composer died, over two hundred years ago.

Among Bach's most famous compositions are: *The Passion According to St. Matthew,* the B Minor Mass, the six *Brandenburg* Concertos,

114

the Concerto for Two Violins, the *Well-Tempered Clavier,* the Prelude and Fugue for Organ in G Minor, the four Suites for Orchestra, and the *Art of Fugue.*

Ex. 99   Bach: Concerto for Two Violins in D Minor

George Frederick Handel

George Frederick Handel (1685-1759) was born in Germany in the same year as Bach. He achieved, however, his greatest successes in Italy and England. Like many of his contemporaries, Handel was a prolific composer, who wrote suites, concertos, choral compositions, and orchestral works, of which the best known are the *Royal Fireworks Music* and the *Water Music.*

In the early eighteenth century, Italian operas were based on intricate mythological plots and staged in lavish fashion with gaudy costumes and elaborate stage machinery. Handel wrote no fewer than forty such Italian operas, which, at first, brought him great success. When the English public tired of the artificiality of these stage spectacles, Handel turned to the composing of oratorios with Biblical themes. Many of his oratorios are known for vigorous and brilliant writing for chorus and orchestra. The most stirring of Handel's great oratorios are *Judas Maccabeus, Israel in Egypt,* and, of course, *The Messiah.*

Joseph Haydn

Joseph Haydn (1732-1809), the son of a poor peasant, came from the Austrian province of Croatia. He worked for many years as the house musician of Prince Esterházy, for whose court he wrote hundreds of melodic, tightly-woven compositions. Besides many piano works, string quartets, and sonatas, Haydn composed one hundred and four symphonies. His music sparkles with a clarity that has seldom been equalled.

116

The best-known of Haydn's works are the *London, The Clock,* and the *Surprise* symphonies, and the oratorio, *The Creation.*

Ex. 100   Haydn: Minuet from *Surprise* Symphony

Mozart in His Tenth Year

Wolfgang Amadeus Mozart (1756-1791) was born in the little town of Salzburg, Austria. He showed his musical genius by composing music at the age of five, when most children today enter kindergarten. His early works resemble those of Haydn, but later on Mozart's style became more personal, filled with wonderful tenderness and melancholy.

117

Like few other composers, Mozart created masterpieces for both the operatic stage and the symphony orchestra. His Symphony in G Minor (No. 40) and *Jupiter* Symphony (No. 41) are magically beautiful works, and his operas, *The Marriage of Figaro, Don Giovanni,* and *The Magic Flute,* are still favorites in the operatic repertoire. One of the greatest of musical geniuses, Mozart suffered a breakdown in health and died tragically at the age of thirty-five.

Ex. 101   Mozart: Symphony No. 40, in G Minor

Ludwig van Beethoven (1770-1827) was the first composer in history who succeeded in writing his music free from external constraint. Until his time, a musician had to compose under the watchful eye of the noble patron or churchman who employed him. Imbued with the ideas of the French Revolution, Beethoven asserted his complete independence as an artist, although he did permit noblemen of Vienna to compete for the honor of supporting him.

As uncompromising in his music as he was in his life, Beethoven brought an explosive energy to the thirty-two piano sonatas and the nine symphonies that he wrote. He also composed piano and violin concertos, an opera, *Fidelio,* and many other works.

Beethoven humanized the old forms, introducing a peasant robustness, violent outbursts of sound, quick changes of mood—from laughter to melancholy. For all his stormy emotions, Beethoven was a master of structure.

Although he became deaf early in life, he heard music with an "inner ear." He continued to develop his powerful and unique style, expressing his thoughts in seventeen remarkable string quartets. Far in advance of the times, Beethoven's last quartets were thought to be

Ludwig van Beethoven

the work of a madman. Now, more than one hundred and thirty years after the composer's death, Beethoven is considered one of the greatest composers the world has ever known.

Ex. 102   Beethoven: Symphony No. 7

Franz Schubert (1797-1828) was a composer of the early Romantic school. His music was often highly personal, emphasizing emotional and dramatic qualities—sometimes at the expense of structure. Schubert's wonderful gift for melody found expression in more than five hundred

Franz Schubert

songs. The piano compositions, the lovely chamber music, and the eight symphonies—especially the famous *Unfinished* Symphony—are filled with warm, singing themes, poetic moods, and dramatic contrasts.

Ex. 103   Schubert: Moment Musical

120

Louis Hector Berlioz

Louis Hector Berlioz (1803-1869), a colorful and dramatic figure in the history of French music, was a leader of the Romantic movement. He wrote some of the earliest and finest examples of program music for orchestra. In instrumentation and in orchestration, Berlioz had no peer, achieving striking dramatic effects, big climaxes, and sharp changes of mood. He used masses of instruments, and introduced rich tone colors and new sonorities into the orchestral sound.

The *Fantastic* Symphony is an arresting and original composition. Through a series of wild escapades, fantastic dreams, and bizarre tableaux, the story reflects the experiences of the composer in the search for his beloved. But more exciting than the narrative is the music itself with its dramatic changes, sensuous tone colors, and flamboyant rhythms.

Other well-known works by Berlioz are *Harold in Italy, Romeo and Juliet,* the *Roman Carnival* Overture, and the *Requiem.*

Felix Mendelssohn

Felix Mendelssohn (1809-1847), German by birth, found inspiration for his music in the landscape and the atmosphere of many countries. Note the titles of some of his compositions—*Scotch* Symphony, *Italian* Symphony, *Venetian Boat Song.* The incidental music, written for Shakespeare's *A Midsummer Night's Dream,* exemplifies Mendelssohn's gift for evoking moods of airy lightness and enchantment.

Though his subject matter is Romantic, Mendelssohn's music reveals Classical precision, transparency, and elegance of form. His *Songs Without Words* and the Concerto in G Minor (both for piano), the oratorio *Elijah,* and the Violin Concerto in E Minor are other well-known works by the composer.

Frédéric Chopin (1810-1849), born of Polish and French parents, was primarily interested in one instrument—the piano. Taking advantage of the rich sonorities made possible by the use of the newly invented pedal, Chopin developed fresh techniques in the art of writing

Frédéric Chopin

for the piano. Widely spaced chords, chromatic harmonies, and brilliant runs mark his style. His compositions are rich in mood and dazzling in sound. Delicate, poetic passages and stormy, surging climaxes are often found in the same work.

Chopin's music combines grace and power; if his imagination was that of a Romantic, his sense of form was that of a Classicist. Outstanding among his many works are Polish-sounding mazurkas and polonaises, Parisian-sounding waltzes, and nocturnes, preludes, études, ballades, and scherzos that know no fatherland.

Ex. 104   Chopin: Nocturne in E Flat

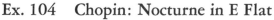

Robert Schumann and his wife, Clara

Robert Schumann (1810-1856) was an early leader in the German Romantic school of composers. His music and his writings typify the Romantic viewpoint—that art springs from the inner moods and impulses of the artist; that the style and the form of music should reflect the personal experience of the composer. Many of Schumann's compositions bear poetic, unexpected names—"Whims," "Soaring," "Sphinxes," "Why?"

In addition to such well-known piano works as *Carnaval, Kreisleriana,* and Fantasy in C Major, Schumann composed some of the best-loved lieder (art songs) and song cycles in the German language. Although his compositions that were written in the short forms are considered his finest, Schumann's chamber music works and his four symphonies contain many passages of great beauty.

124

Richard Wagner

Richard Wagner (1813-1883), born in Leipzig, Germany, was the first great composer to possess the diverse gifts of dramatist, critic, theater director, and man of action. Objecting to the artificiality of grand opera, he tried to supplant it with a new type of musical work called "music drama."

Wagner's music dramas include *Tristan and Isolde, Parsifal, The Mastersingers of Nuremberg,* and a set of four operas that tell a continuous story, *The Ring of the Nibelung.* In all these works the orchestra is just as important as are the singers. It introduces the "leitmotifs"— short themes which are played whenever a certain character appears on stage or when an important topic is mentioned. Wagner's orchestration is brilliantly sensuous, and the listener can enjoy the orchestral passages in his music dramas even without hearing the vocal parts that belong with them.

The composer wrote his own opera stories, or "librettos," adapting these from old German legends. He also persuaded the King of Bavaria and other admirers to build an opera house in Bayreuth, Germany, for the performance of his works. His music dramas are still played there today, and people from all over the world go to the Wagner Festivals to hear them.

Ex. 105   Wagner: The Ride of the Valkyries, from *The Valkyrie*

Johannes Brahms

Johannes Brahms (1833-1897) was born in Hamburg, Germany. In his music he combined the warm, personal quality of the Romantic style with the power of traditional forms. His many songs and short piano pieces reveal the intimate, poetic side of his nature.

126

Some of Brahms' compositions, such as the famous "Lullaby," are reminiscent of German folk music. Alternately dramatic and warmly lyrical, his concertos for violin and for piano, and his four symphonies are found among the most frequently performed orchestral works today.

Ex. 106   Brahms: Symphony No. 2

Modeste Moussorgsky

Modeste Moussorgsky (1839-1881), wrote realistic, strong, and deeply Russian music. Living among the peasants, he wove into his compositions the roughness, the earthy quality, the unusual scales, and the vital rhythms of Russian folk music. His works are few, but each one carries the flavor of the countryside and of the life he saw around him. Among Moussorgsky's best-known works are the tragic opera *Boris Godunov; A Night on Bald Mountain,* orchestrated by Rimsky-Korsakoff; and a piano suite *Pictures at an Exhibition,* orchestrated by Maurice Ravel.

Ex. 107   Moussorgsky: *Pictures at an Exhibition*

127

Peter Ilyich Tchaikovsky

Peter Ilyich Tchaikovsky (1840-1893). The name, Tchaikovsky, calls to mind his sweeping, singing melodies. A master of orchestration, the Russian composer caught the color and the mood of his native landscape in many of his compositions. Behind the gay, lively themes, there often lurks a touch of melancholy.

His most popular works include the *Nutcracker* Suite; Fantasy Overture *Romeo and Juliet; The Swan Lake* ballet; and the Fourth, the Fifth, and the Sixth symphonies. Tchaikovsky's Violin Concerto in D Major and the Piano Concerto in B Flat Minor are important compositions in the concerto repertoire.

Ex. 108   Tchaikovsky: Symphony No. 5

128

Giuseppe Verdi

Giuseppe Verdi (1813-1901), greatest Italian opera composer in the nineteenth century, lived to be eighty-eight and continued to grow as an artist until very near the end of his life. His music was so popular in his country that his name became a household word. Verdi had a superb sense of theater. Although some of the stories he set to music seem old-fashioned today, his operas are repeatedly performed, stirring the audience with their fire and thunder. Verdi was a man obsessed by a strong love of freedom, and some of his operas were thinly veiled pleas for the liberation of his homeland, then ruled by Austria.

Among his many well-known operas are *Rigoletto, Il Trovatore, La Traviata, Don Carlos,* and *Aïda. Falstaff* and *Otello,* written when Verdi was over seventy years old, were composed in a tightly-knit style. They are considered his best works, remarkable for their musical vitality and dramatic effectiveness.

Ex. 109   Verdi: Farewell Now to the Memories, from *La Traviata*

Fare - well now, — to the love-ly mem - 'ries, — to the world of pleas- ure, — fad - ing fast a - way. —

Giacomo Puccini (1858-1924) was one of the last in the line of Italy's great opera composers. Gifted with a rich melodic power and a strong sense of theater, Puccini had a unique talent for creating a character through music. His operas possess popular appeal and yet afford lasting interest to the discriminating musician.

A Romantic to the core, Puccini wrote with affection and understanding for the human voice. He was influenced by the *verismo* (realistic) school. His music displayed a startling melodramatic quality—the torture scene in *Tosca;* the suicide of Cho-cho-san in *Madame Butterfly;* and the execution of the unfortunate suitors in *Turandot.* Ardent lyricism, sharp contrasts of mood, exotic stage effects, lively crowd scenes, and rapid changes from tragedy to comedy characterize Puccini's genius.

The composer was at his best in writing music that portrayed tender, star-crossed lovers: Mimi and Rodolfo in *La Bohème;* Tosca and Cavaradossi in *Tosca;* Pinkerton and Cho-cho-san in *Madame Butterfly.* Most of his operas won immediate success, and their appeal to audiences all over the world remains undiminished to this day.

7

Twentieth-Century Music

Every period in history has created its own musical style. In the Middle Ages, religious choral music prevailed; in the nineteenth century, Romantic music; in the twentieth century—for want of a better name—"modern" music.

Modern Music

To certain people, the word "modern" suggests music that is wild, noisy, or chaotic. This is a one-sided view, for some twentieth-century music is warm, tender, and stirring. Present-day composers differ sharply from one another in their styles and techniques, and each composer should be judged solely on his own merits.

A frequent criticism of modern music is that it has no melody. Some twentieth-century composers seem unwilling to write a singing line. But if you listen to the works of Prokofiev, Honegger, Milhaud, Revueltas, or Villa-Lobos, you will hear modern music that is full of melody.

Modern melodies are freer and more adventurous than the old ones. At times they jump about unexpectedly, as is characteristic of our energetic century of planes, jets, and rockets.

This free motion can be exhilarating, as it is heard, for instance, in the main theme of *Peter and the Wolf*.

Ex. 110   Prokofiev: *Peter and the Wolf*

Complex rhythm is another striking feature of modern music. Not only do present-day composers write measures with varying numbers of beats—9/4, 5/8, 7/16, etc.—but they also write odd rhythmic patterns within the measure. Offbeat rhythms, cross-accents, and other interesting rhythmical devices increase the intensity and power of many modern compositions. Bartók, Stravinsky, Milhaud, Ives, and Copland are among those modern composers who have developed distinctive rhythmic patterns in their works.

A third feature of modern music is its bold use of timbres and orchestral colors. In order to produce unusual sonority, a composer, for example, may choose the piercing, highest notes of the clarinet, piccolo, or trumpet, or he may use the growling, lowest notes of the French horn or of the double bass. He may obtain a weird effect with a hollow sound—a melody in the high piccolo, another in the contrabassoon, and nothing between.

"Dissonances," a striking quality of modern music, are chords in which tones clash, instead of blend. When concertgoers first heard modern dissonances, many of them gritted their teeth and marched out of the hall. Now, so many of these chords are used in the background music for films and television plays that they no longer sound awkward or disturbing.

When heard frequently, dissonances have a strange way of becoming "consonances"—harmonious chords. The true composer uses modern harmonies not for the purpose of startling the audience but for expressing his ideas and emotions.

Present-day music has a new kind of tonality. Classical music always started and ended in the same key, all instruments—or, in piano music, both hands—playing in that key. One often hears the expression, "Sonata in C Major," which means that the sonata starts and ends in the key of C Major.

Certain composers, Shostakovich and Milhaud among them, may write a composition in which two different tonalities can be heard at the same time. To use the piano as example, the music for the right hand may be written in the key of A Major, and the music for the accompaniment—the left hand—written in the key of E Flat Minor. Does this kind of music make sense? Of course it does, when it is the work of a good composer. It resembles the technique used by the modern author to describe a person experiencing two different emotions simultaneously.

A favorite among modern compositions, Stravinsky's *Petroushka,* makes use of this two-keys-at-a-time kind of writing—"polytonality." This has become a common technique in modern music. For an example of polytonality, see More About Harmony, in Chapter 9.

Another new method of writing music is known as "atonality"— music without a key. This technique, originated by Arnold Schönberg, has quite a number of champions, and has influenced such composers as Alban Berg and Anton von Webern. If you wish to hear some atonal music, listen to Schönberg's *Five Pieces for Orchestra* or Berg's Violin Concerto.

Modern music has its challengers as well as its champions. Not too long ago, a critic wrote a book to prove that modern composers were failures, and that they might very well give up writing since no one understood or cared for their music.

Of course, not all modern works are great masterpieces, and the music of certain twentieth-century composers is quite difficult to grasp. The same criticism, however, may be made of the music of every age. Many of the works of Bach, Beethoven, Moussorgsky, and other famous composers were difficult to understand when they were first written. Bach's *Art of Fugue* and Beethoven's late string quartets still require considerable study before they can be fully enjoyed. The difficulty or the simplicity of a composition is not a measure of its worth. Some music is light and easy; other music is packed with ideas that require attention and repeated hearing. But the satisfaction such music can give makes the effort of careful listening worth while.

Current record catalogs contain pages and pages of listings of modern music. Apparently hundreds of thousands, if not millions, of people are buying records of Bartók, Prokofiev, Milhaud, Hindemith, Copland, Villa-Lobos, Gershwin, Shostakovich, and other contemporaries.

Although a great many people prefer the classics, the audience for modern music is steadily growing. Modern music has many branches, many different styles. Some compositions will endure, some will be forgotten, but to the development of the art, modern music is making a rich contribution.

Great Modern Composers

In music, as in other arts, the "moderns" of one generation become the "classics" of the next. When I was a young piano student, I remember the enthusiasm with which I greeted my teacher's announcement that he would permit me to play a work of "that French modernist," Claude Debussy. Today, of course, Debussy's music is widely accepted. It is played in public parks, and is piped into those elegant restaurants where the waiters tread softly and the music is meant to be a background for conversation.

Here are brief biographies of some of the twentieth-century composers whose works, considered radical yesterday, are accepted masterpieces today.

134

Claude Debussy

Claude Debussy (1862-1918), the famous French composer, was a pioneer in twentieth-century music. He had an extremely sensitive ear, and developed a whole range of subtle harmonies that broke ground for many modern developments—for example, indefinite tonality. Debussy was fascinated by the problems of creating music that was delicate, transparent, and poetic. The titles of some of his works, *Clouds, Mists, Bells Through the Leaves,* suggest the mingled pastel colors of impressionist paintings by Monet or Renoir. Much of his music seems hushed and dreamlike in mood—especially so in *Clair de Lune (Moonlight),* the Nocturnes, and *The Afternoon of a Faun.*

Ex. 111 Debussy: *The Afternoon of a Faun*

Maurice Ravel (1875-1937), another noted French composer, possessed a marked gift for creating original harmonies and striking orchestration. His music has clear-cut form, and is often witty, with touches of satire. He wrote many piano compositions and orchestral works. Some of his major works are *Daphnis and Chloë, La Valse,* and *Bolero*

Maurice Ravel

for orchestra; two piano concertos; *Tzigane* for violin and piano; and the delightful children's piece *Mother Goose* Suite.

Ex. 112   Ravel: *Pavane*

Igor Stravinsky (1882-   ) was born in Russia, lived for many years in France, and then became an American citizen. Between 1911 and 1917 he started a musical revolution with his daring use of dissonances, cross-rhythms, and powerful orchestral colors. He has continued to compose works in various forms, such as the opera *The Rake's Progress,* the Symphony in C, and the *Symphony of Psalms.* His early compositions, based on Russian themes, however, make the strongest impression on audiences today. In addition to *The Fire Bird, Petroushka,* and *The Rite of Spring,* Stravinsky has written *The Story of a Soldier, The Wedding,* and the symphonic poem *Song of the Nightingale.*

136

Igor Stravinsky

Ex. 113   Stravinsky: *The Rite of Spring*

Arnold Schönberg (1874-1951), Vienna born, inventor of atonality and of the twelve-tone system, was one of the most provocative figures in contemporary music. His harmony made an almost complete break with the past, and influenced a great number of composers. Those who are not used to Schönberg's style may find his works extremely difficult listening. But his compositions are never boring—one either loves them or hates them!

For an introduction to Schönberg's music, listen to his *Transfigured Night, Gürrelieder,* and *Pierrot Lunaire.*

Ernst Toch (1887-   ) has successfully combined a fresh, modern style with rich, romantic feeling. His writing is bold, yet lyrical, as befits a composer born in Vienna and related emotionally to Mozart, Schubert, and Brahms. Toch's compositions include *The Chinese Flute; Pinocchio, a Merry Overture;* the fairy tale opera *The Princess on the Pea;* many chamber music works; and five symphonies.

Paul Hindemith (1895-   ) born in Germany, is a brilliant and productive modern composer. His music is noted for its masterful and logical construction. Since many of his compositions are quite complex, they require repeated hearings. Hindemith has evolved an original type of dissonant counterpoint, revealing at times the influence of an earlier German contrapuntalist, J. S. Bach. A few of the important compositions in Hindemith's vast list are *Matthias the Painter; Symphonic Metamorphosis on Themes by Weber;* Chamber Music, Op. 24, No. 2; and the short satirical opera *There and Back.*

Serge Prokofiev

Serge Prokofiev (1891-1953) was one of the greatest of Russian composers. Everyone seems to know his musical fairy tale, *Peter and the Wolf.* He brought back into modern music a warm sense of melody, a quality that had been largely neglected by other moderns. Prokofiev's music is also well known for its humor. Such works as *Love for Three Oranges* and *Lieutenant Kijé* Suite reflect his interest in the satirical and the grotesque.

Prokofiev's compositions have great brilliance and clarity, and some of his works, the cantata *Alexander Nevsky,* for instance, display extraordinary dramatic power. The *Classical* Symphony, two violin concertos, five piano concertos, and the superb Fifth Symphony are representative of his work.

Ex. 114   Prokofiev: Gavotte, from *Classical* Symphony

Béla Bartók

Béla Bartók (1881-1945), famous Hungarian composer, spent many years collecting old Hungarian folk songs. A believer in freedom, he fled his native land when Hitler invaded it, and came to the United States. In the midst of writing one of his greatest works, the Viola Concerto, he died. After his death, Bartók's music began to be widely performed, earning the money he had so desperately needed during his lifetime. Bartók's compositions are strong, harsh, often dissonant, and make use

139

of many of the folk melodies he uncovered. Among his works are *Mikrokosmos* for piano, six string quartets, three piano concertos, and the beautiful Concerto for Orchestra.

Ex. 115   Bartók: Concerto for Orchestra

Arthur Honegger

Arthur Honegger (1892-1955), Swiss-born composer, lived in France most of his life. A member of the group of musical rebels called "Les Six," Honegger excelled in compositions of a robust, dramatic character. He experimented with a typically modern kind of realism in *Pacific 231,* a musical portrait of a railroad train. His *Chant de Joie (Song of Joy)* makes use of dissonance in an exhilarating, powerful manner. Honegger composed five symphonies, several operas, and many chamber music works; his most successful compositions were the oratorios, *King David* and *Joan of Arc at the Stake.*

140

Darius Milhaud

Darius Milhaud (1892-   ) is a vigorous and down-to-earth French composer. He wrote one of the first—and still one of the best—pieces of jazz in classical form, *The Creation of the World*. His *Suite Française,* written for high-school bands, presents a fresh and brilliant treatment of French folk music. Milhaud likes to use folk songs, music hall tunes, and lively dissonances in his music. His compositions include the operas, *Christophe Colombe, Maximilien, Bolivar,* and *David;* concertos for piano, violin, and other instruments; eighteen string quartets; orchestral suites; and nine symphonies. Among his well-known works are the *Sacred Service; The Poor Sailor,* a short opera; and *Le Boeuf sur le Toit,* literally translated "the ox on the roof," but known in English as *The Nothing Doing Bar.*

Ex. 116   Milhaud: *Suite Française*

Dmitri Shostakovich

Dmitri Shostakovich (1906-   ), famous Soviet Russian composer, is probably the greatest living master of the symphony. Creating his First Symphony at the age of eighteen, he has now written eleven works in this form. His music has two qualities that are rare among modern composers—heroic style and great emotional depth. Although Shostakovich makes use of many dissonances and other modern devices, his dramatic line has meaning for even the untrained listener. He has written many works, including eight string quartets, a quintet for piano and strings, and concertos for piano, violin, and cello. Among his most important compositions are his First, Fifth, and Tenth symphonies.

Ex. 117   Shostakovich: Symphony No. 5

Charles Ives (1874-1954), American-born composer, worked in the insurance business by day and wrote his music at night. He was a daring and original composer. His compositions are often quite dissonant and

142

unconventional in structure. They merge many disparate elements—old New England hymn tunes, country dances, polytonal harmonies, and ragtime rhythms—into a uniquely "Ivesian" style.

Ives' two piano sonatas and his four sonatas for violin and piano are touched with strong Yankee vitality. *The Housatonic at Stockbridge* and *The Unanswered Question* are among his most interesting orchestral works. His one hundred and fourteen songs cover an amazing variety of moods, ranging from the raucous "Walt Whitman" and the satirical "Down with the Politicians and Up with the People," to the delicate "The Nightingale" and the mystical "Serenity."

Many of his innovations foreshadowed the music of the European modernists. Although Ives' works are rarely heard, his reputation as an important American composer is steadily growing.

Ex. 118   Ives: Charlie Rutlage

An - oth - er good cow-punch-er has gone to meet his fate.

George Gershwin (1898-1937) achieved many "firsts" during his comparatively short life. He was the first to write successfully in both the popular and the classical fields; he was the first American to introduce jazz into the serious musical forms; and he was the first American composer to win world-wide popularity. Throughout his career, he continued to study and to develop as a composer.

Among Gershwin's famous compositions are the *Rhapsody in Blue;* Concerto in F, for piano and orchestra; and *An American in Paris.* His show tunes, "Lady Be Good," "The Man I Love," "I Got Rhythm," " 'Swonderful," and others, have not been surpassed in melodic appeal

George Gershwin

and rhythmic freshness. His masterpiece, the opera *Porgy and Bess,* has been performed in all the important opera houses in the world except, ironically enough, the Metropolitan Opera in New York.

Aaron Copland (1900-   ) is a distinguished and widely recognized American composer. His style is spare and clear, and modern. He often weaves jazz rhythms and folk elements into his work, creating music of originality and good taste.

In addition to composing, Copland is a vigorous champion of the works of American composers, and has done much to win for them the acceptance that many still lack. He has composed in many forms, from chamber music and symphonies to music for ballet, radio, films, and opera *(The Tender Land).* Besides possessing a brilliant and distinctive rhythmic sense, Copland also has a great flair for orchestration, as shown in his works: *El Salon Mexico, Billy the Kid, Rodeo, Appalachian Spring,* and the Third Symphony.

144

8

American Music

The beginnings of American music date back to colonial times when the earliest folk songs, such as "Springfield Mountain," appeared. The Revolutionary hymns of William Billings and the genteel art songs of Francis Hopkinson, a signer of the Declaration of Independence, were, probably, the first compositions written in this country.

For over one hundred years, the conflicts and growing pains of the nation left little time for the development of original serious American music. But the joys and the sorrows of the people found rich expression in a vast body of folk and popular songs. The tunes of the early minstrel bands in the 1840's already revealed traces of syncopation. A decade later, Stephen Foster created the ballads that were the first native music to make the reverse journey across the sea.

After the Civil War an outburst of new, distinctly American songs appeared—Negro spirituals, cowboy ballads, songs of Mississippi boatmen, and songs of railroaders, such as "Casey Jones." The Gay Nineties brought forth a flood of "tear-jerkers," overly sentimental songs in three-quarter time. At the turn of the century, ragtime appeared with its brisk offbeat accents that sent America dancing.

Toward the end of the nineteenth century and at the beginning of the twentieth, a number of serious composers were writing music in the large forms. The works of Horatio Parker, Edward MacDowell, Charles Griffes, and Charles Martin Loeffler were skillfully written, showing talent but no great originality.

It was jazz that brought a breath of fresh air into American music, and it was jazz that first made the world sit up and take notice that America was capable of producing a new, impudent, distinctive music of its own.

Jazz

Jazz owes much to the folk music of many countries. Settlers from England, Ireland, France, Spain, and slaves from Africa brought their music to America. In the beginning, each group sang its own songs. About 1900, the various types of folk music had intermingled, and a new kind of music was born—jazz.

Anyone who spends even one day in the United States is bound to hear jazz in one form or another. Can jazz be defined? One minute of listening to jazz is worth more than a month of explanation. Since no two people would agree on the same definition for jazz, it is better to discuss some of the elements found in this kind of music.

I would say that jazz has five characteristic qualities: (1) its rhythm, (2) the special way it is played or sung, (3) the blues scale, (4) the jazz band, and (5) jazz improvisation.

A basic part of jazz rhythm is the steady, pulsating underbeat. No matter what else is going on in the music, at least one of the instruments —the bass, the drums, the cymbal, or the guitar—plays this continuous beat throughout the number. The beat may shift from one instrument to another, or it may stop for a moment (this is called a "break"). But the beat starts again and keeps on going, usually to the very end.

Over this basic beat, other instruments play the tune, usually introducing offbeat accents and syncopations. The melody keeps on shifting and changing its rhythm, always coming up with surprises. Rhythmic variety is one of the delights of good jazz.

A true jazz musician does not sing or play with the same kind of tone as does his classical brother. Instead of a sustained, pure tone, the

146

jazz singer or instrumentalist tends to perform with a throbbing, vibrant sound that often slides up to and around the note. When a jazz tone sounds off pitch, it probably is intentional. The jazz man plays around the pitch because he can put more jazz quality into the music by doing so.

A jazz trombonist moves the slide of his instrument in and out very slightly and very fast. This motion produces the vibrato or "wobble" that is so much a part of traditional jazz. The trombonist sometimes plays with a rough, "gut-bucket" tone, like the expressive "gravel" voice of a blues shouter. The famous trumpeter, Louis Armstrong, both sings and plays the trumpet that way.

Recently there has been a switch from "hot" to "cool" jazz, and part of the change is in tone quality. Vibrato and the hoarse intensity of early jazz are out-of-date for the "cool" men, who play with an absolutely even, expressionless tone.

The blues is a form of early Negro folk song that has become an integral part of jazz. When playing or singing the blues, the performer tends to make the third and the seventh tones of the scale slightly flat. The slight flatting of the third and the seventh produces the blues scale. This scale, shown here, gives blues music a special flavor of its own. Some people believe that the blues scale originated in Africa, and was brought to America by the early slaves. Another feature of the blues is its twelve-measure phrase—an unusual length for popular songs.

Ex. 119

In the early 1900's, Negro musicians of New Orleans were forming the jazz band. The earliest bands consisted of trumpet, trombone, clarinet, tuba, and drums. Later the tuba was dropped, and the piano and the banjo were added. When jazz traveled up the Mississippi and reached Chicago, the saxophone was included, and then the double bass.

Now, there are many types of jazz bands. A familiar type has three sections: (1) reeds—the clarinet and the saxophone; (2) brass—a trumpet or two, and often a trombone; (3) rhythm—the drums, the piano, the double bass, and, sometimes, the guitar.

No other sound is quite like that of a jazz band. Although some people consider it loud and tinny, other people are "sent"—excited—by the jazz band. But whatever value is placed on it, fans and critics, alike, agree that jazz has carved a comfortable niche for itself in American life.

The last, and possibly the most distinctive feature of jazz, is improvisation. Improvising music means inventing it spontaneously as it is being performed.

A jazz improvisation is almost always based on a well-known song, such as "I Got Rhythm" or "How High the Moon," but a true jazz musician never plays the tune exactly as it is written. He will vary the rhythm, add or omit notes of the melody, and make other changes. What is almost always retained is the underlying chord pattern of the original song. Often the tune being played is so changed that it is scarcely recognizable. To the jazz man it is not the tune but what he adds to the tune that matters.

Frequently, three or four instrumentalists will improvise together on the same tune, each playing his own musical pattern. A "jam session" such as this can be a vital and creative experience. Sometimes the players perform a kind of jazz counterpoint, a refreshing and exciting form of music.

Jazz is now more than fifty years old. Its style has changed a number of times, and it is still changing. The earliest jazz style was New Orleans marching jazz—music played from about 1890 to 1920 for weddings, funerals, and political rallies by Negro street bands. That variety of jazz was energetic, wild, and raucous.

Overlapping and mingling with marching jazz was "Dixieland"—a type of ragtime for five instruments, with drums and tuba playing the beat, and clarinet, trumpet, and trombone improvising freely. The instruments played a rough counterpoint with frequently clashing tones, much syncopation, and thin, piercing quality. Louis Armstrong's trumpet playing and Jellyroll Morton's piano improvisations were features of this period. Characteristic tunes were "When the Saints Go Marching In" and "Muskrat Ramble."

About 1909, W. C. Handy wrote the first blues song. In 1913 the "St. Louis Blues" was published. Well-known blues singers, such as Bessie Smith and Ma Rainey, took this shouting, wavering, sensuous music throughout the South, and soon jazz musicians began to play the blues on trumpet and trombone.

As jazz went upriver from New Orleans to St. Louis, Chicago, and Kansas City, it was gradually becoming polished. Musicians (Bix Beiderbecke was one of them) played with refined tone, and even rehearsed their performances. When jazz reached New York, arrangers, such as Fletcher Henderson, appeared, and the era of written jazz and the big band started.

By about 1935 swing had taken over. Big, well-rehearsed bands played elaborately harmonized arrangements of popular songs. Instrumentalists, among them Benny Goodman on clarinet, Harry James on trumpet, and Gene Krupa on drums, developed brilliant jazz virtuosity. Improvisation was now allocated to the soloist, while everyone else played from written music.

The big bands began to break up around 1945, and the small "combo" of three or four men returned with a new, wilder kind of improvisation. It was named "bebop," or simply "bop," and its leaders were trumpeter "Dizzy" Gillespie, and saxophonist Charlie Parker. Bop is highly irregular, almost hysterical jazz, with a very fast beat, choppy counter-rhythms, and a melodic line broken into fragments. "Bopsters" use modern harmonies that they learned by listening to the music of

Hindemith, Bartók, and other modern composers. Bop brought jazz to a state of near frenzy.

Another branch in the development of jazz is the "cool" movement. Working in small combos, Dave Brubeck, Miles Davis, Gerry Mulligan, and Lennie Tristano, among others, have introduced a restrained, dead-pan note into jazz. Cool players seem almost indifferent when they play. Their tone is cold and detached, their accents are subtle, the rhythmic pulse is light and delicate, and the melody has virtually disappeared. Cool pieces are often contrapuntal, almost intellectual, and many cool jazz men, including Brubeck, Jimmy Guiffre, and John Lewis of the Modern Jazz Quartet, are well-trained and serious musicians.

Whatever changes have taken place in it, jazz continues to hold the interest of millions of people throughout the world, with many fine musicians among them. European composers—Stravinsky, Ravel, Milhaud, Honegger, Hindemith, and others—have used jazz, and many American composers have made it a basic ingredient in their larger compositions.

More American Music

In addition to folk music and jazz, this country has given two other types of American music to the world: popular songs and American concert music. For over thirty years, song writers, such as Harold Arlen, Irving Berlin, George Gershwin, Jerome Kern, Cole Porter, and Richard Rodgers, have created a vast repertoire of lively, sophisticated, or sentimental tunes that the whole world sings. From the twenties through the forties, composers brought forth a rich harvest of popular songs in great variety, many of them filled with fresh melodic or rhythmic turns.

Popular music and jazz complement each other. Progressive jazz men, though they scorn commercial song arrangements, cannot do without the lifeblood of popular tunes. Nor can the bands that play popular music reject for long the constantly changing ways of playing that the *avant garde* of jazz makes available to them.

Jazz Quartet

Formerly American composers who created music in the larger forms wrote in the tradition of the European classic masters. As long as the conservatory-trained American musicians had their thoughts exclusively fixed on Europe, their works had a pale, imitative quality.

When, in the early years of this century, a number of composers made contact with the musical world of the American streets, theater, dance halls, and the vital music of native tradition, our serious music entered a new and lively phase. Just as writers before them—men such as Walt Whitman, Mark Twain, Theodore Dreiser, Carl Sandburg, and

Sinclair Lewis—drew a rough-grained vigor from common American speech and ways of living, composers—such as Ives, Gershwin, Copland, and Harris—began to write a new kind of serious music. This trend was enlivened by the tunes and rhythms of the Negro, the cowboy, jazz, the square dance, and the polyglot, earthy American scene.

The movement for serious American music gathered momentum in the 1920's, and has continued to develop at an increasing pace in the past three decades. Composers have created a great number of sonatas, symphonies, ballet and film scores, operas, and chamber music, in a distinctly American idiom.

Jazz rhythms and melodic patterns color the music of such men as Leonard Bernstein, Marc Blitzstein, Aaron Copland, Morton Gould, George Kleinsinger, Meyer Kupferman, Jerome Moross, Alex North, and Gunther Schuller. Folklike rhythms, melodies, and scales are clearly evident in the works of Henry Cowell, Lukas Foss, Roy Harris, Bernard Herrmann, Douglas Moore, and Virgil Thomson.

The mingling of popular style and serious form is creating a new kind of music in this country, as did similar trends in past centuries in Italy, Germany, Russia, and other nations.

Not all American composers, however, are influenced by folk music or jazz. Many distinguished musical figures of today—among them

152

Samuel Barber, Paul Creston, Norman Dello Joio, David Diamond, Howard Hanson, Leon Kirchner, Gian-Carlo Menotti, Walter Piston, Wallingford Riegger, William Schuman, Roger Sessions—have worked in a diversity of styles that are related to those of leading European composers.

American music is young, and its future is unpredictable. It will be interesting to observe its course in the years to come.

How a Composer Works

Although they differ in many ways, most composers possess certain qualities—a love for music, an urge to write, talent, a command of the skills of composition, patience, and the ability and the willingness to work hard.

No one knows where a composer finds a musical idea, a melody, or a rhythm. Possibly it comes from the music he heard when very young, or from his moods, his thoughts, random associations, or musical experiments. Some composers find melodies floating into their heads at unexpected times—while taking a bath, playing chess, or riding in the subway. Some hear music in dreams. But, most frequently, ideas come to the composer when he works at his piano, or at his desk, or when he paces up and down the room.

My day usually starts with improvising. I play the piano, and let ideas come into my mind, waiting for something to happen. If I am lucky, something does happen. I start by writing down a line or two of a melody, or a group of chords, or some mere fragments of music. After jotting down three or four pages of such tentative beginnings, one idea suddenly seems fresh and interesting. Quickly, I set down twenty or thirty measures that have possibilities.

Then comes "deadwood." But I write it all down in any case, having learned from experience that this is not the time to evaluate the work.

Stopping for a while, I may write a letter, or prepare plans for an orchestra concert I am to conduct a few months later. Returning to the piano in a "cold" mood, I play over what I have written. Delighted with the good measures and annoyed with the miserable ones, I cut, change, and rewrite. Perhaps the melody is repetitious or the harmonies static. Then come more revisions, alterations, and possibly the rewriting of parts of the sketch two or three times. On good days things go quickly. I sketched out *Ozark Set,* for instance, in less than a week.

On bad days, I cannot find an ending for a movement, or an idea for a third movement to complete the two already written. This is the time to lay the work aside, and to let it "ripen" for a week, a month, or longer, and start on something else. At the moment there are seven or eight uncompleted works lying on the piano waiting to be finished, among them an opera, cello sonata, a symphony, music for a play, two piano sonatinas in jazz, a sketch for a piano concerto, and various odds and ends. Which composition will be completed first, and which will never be completed, remain for the future to decide.

What often settles such problems is either a sudden burst of enthusiasm, or a request to finish a composition by a certain date. The knowledge that a conductor or producer is waiting for music, that he will perform it or use it in a play or film, is a wonderful stimulus for the composer to complete a work in progress.

One of my happiest times came during the writing of Symphony No. 1—Leopold Stokowski wanted a finished score for a particular performance by the New York Philharmonic. Another such occasion was the writing of the music for the film, *They Came to Cordura.* Composing with a stop watch in hand to meet the precise timings of the completed film, I found the dramatic images exciting, and was able to finish the hour-long score in five weeks.

I do not know how musical ideas spring up. Much of the composer's work is thinking, organizing, and planning what to do with his material. For example, when a composer finds a theme his first concern is how to use it. For what kind of composition would such a theme be suitable? Piano music, chamber music, or orchestral composition? What form should the music take? Which instrument or instruments would be most appropriate?

Modern String Quartet

To solve such problems, the composer needs experience and training. His past work in music, his knowledge of the compositions of others, the techniques he has developed—all these help him to find solutions.

Every composer has his own methods of procedure, certain musical principles that he follows in writing his music. Bach used a highly-organized counterpoint that obeyed harmonic laws; Wagner strove to combine operatic and symphonic methods; Debussy sought for transparent orchestral colors floating in a harmonic mist. The combination of favorite techniques and personal turns of expression are what is termed the "style" of a composer.

In recent times, some composers have felt the need to formalize their styles into definite systems of writing music. Some of these are the Schillinger system, the twelve-tone system of Schönberg, Hindemith's system, and, more recently, the electronic or "concrete" music systems of Karlheinz Stockhausen and of Pierre Boulez.

Other composers, Ives, Milhaud, and Prokofiev, among them, have refrained from formalizing their methods. Perhaps they feel that composing by the rules of such "systems" is constraining, and prefer the freedom of allowing the imagination to flow unhampered.

All composers are deeply indebted to the masters who preceded them and to the great composers of the present. Like most serious musicians, I study constantly; and I try to learn the secrets of writing great music from the classical composers, and from those moderns whose work I admire.

At certain times my musical ideas seem to fall into exactly the right place. Composing then becomes exciting, and I would not exchange my job for any other I can think of. But what is most important, I believe, is to keep on writing, for each new composition is a search, a battle, a voyage of discovery.

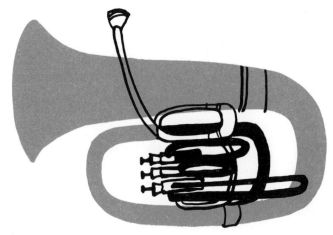

9

More About Music

More About Scales and Keys

Earlier in the book, we discussed the minor scale. Actually, there are three different forms of minor scale in use today—the so-called "natural minor," the "harmonic minor," and the "melodic minor." All three are alike in that each has a half step between the second and third tones of the scale, but after that, they differ from one another. These illustrations show the construction of the three forms of minor scale:

Ex. 120   Natural Minor

Ex. 121   Harmonic Minor

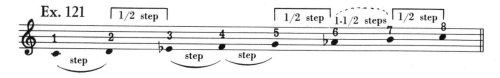

157

The melodic minor is different from other scales because it has one form for going up the scale and another for coming down. Here are the two forms of melodic minor scale:

Ex. 122   Melodic Minor, Rising

Ex. 123   Melodic Minor, Falling

There are many other types of scales, both ancient and modern, each of which has its own character and its own musical possibilities.

Here are a few interesting scales:

Ex. 124   The Phrygian Scale, often used in Spanish music

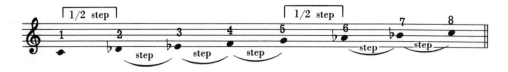

Ex. 125   The Dorian Scale, found in many old English ballads

Ex. 126   The Pentatonic Scale, used by the Chinese

Ex. 127   The Whole Tone Scale,
           borrowed by Debussy from the Javanese

Ex. 128   The Chromatic or Twelve-Tone Scale

More About Harmony

If you want to know more about the structure of chords, here are a few pointers.

In traditional music, chords are built in "thirds."

This is a third, built on C: Another third, built on E:

       Ex. 129a   **Ex. 129b**

159

If the third built on C and the third built on E are put together, one above the other like this:

Ex. 130

a basic chord, called a "triad," is formed. The triad contains three tones: a fundamental, a third, and a fifth.

A similar triad can be built on any step of the scale. Always start with a fundamental, add a third, and then a fifth.

Ex. 131

About the year 1600, composers began to add another third to the triad, thereby creating the "seventh" chord. Seventh chords have four different tones.

Ex. 132 Seventh Chord

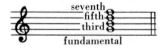

In the nineteenth century, another third was added, and thus the "ninth" chord came into use. It has five tones.

160

Ex. 133   Ninth Chord

Near the beginning of the twentieth century, composers, such as Debussy and Ravel, extended the range of harmony still further. By adding yet another third, they produced a chord with six different tones —the "eleventh" chord.

Ex. 134   Eleventh Chord

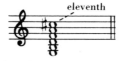

In our own time, many new experiments with harmony have been made. One of these experiments, originated by the Russian composer, Alexander Scriabin, abandoned the traditional idea that chords must be built in thirds. Scriabin developed a new method of chord construction by using "fourths." His chords sounded something like this:

Ex. 135

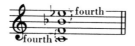

Modern harmony is often very complex. Here is an example of polytonality. The chord in the right hand is in the key of E flat, while the chord in the left hand is in the key of E. The example is from Stravinsky's *The Rite of Spring*.

Ex. 136   Stravinsky: *The Rite of Spring*

A knowledge of harmony—how chords are constructed and their relationships to each other—is essential to a complete understanding of music. Some people have an instinctive grasp of harmony. They can play complicated series of chords by ear, yet not know how to read music. But most people, including many brilliant musicians, must gain this knowledge through study and hard work. Although at least one or two years of concentrated study is needed to understand harmony, such knowledge can prove most rewarding.

More About Counterpoint: The Fugue

One of the most fascinating and challenging forms of music is the fugue. Here, counterpoint requires the greatest degree of concentration from the listener. Many people associate the fugue with the name of Bach. This is not surprising, since no other composer expressed himself so naturally and so freely in this form as did Bach. Because his fugues are beautifully interwoven, varied in expression, and perfect in form, anyone who has learned how to listen to them finds their appeal endless.

Like many other contrapuntal pieces, a fugue starts with a short melody, or subject, that is played or sung by one "voice" without accompaniment. This is the subject of the Fugue No. 1 in Bach's *Well-Tempered Clavier:*

Ex. 137a Bach: *Well-Tempered Clavier,* Fugue No. 1

As soon as the first voice has finished with the subject, the second voice takes it up. This second voice is a fifth (five tones of the scale) higher than the first one.

Ex. 137b

The example shows that when the second voice comes in, the first voice does not stop, but continues, playing a contrasting melody called the "countersubject."

While the two voices continue to spin out their melodic lines, a third voice enters with the original subject. Then the fourth joins in to complete the opening section or "exposition" of the fugue.

Ex. 137c

When all four voices have played the subject in turn, the fugue is well under way and into the development section.

Now the fun really begins. The subject passes from voice to voice, disappearing and reappearing. Now it soars out loud and clear in the top part; now it is heard deep in the bass; here it is in the middle voice with counter melodies all around it. The composer, with his four melodies going at once, is like a juggler keeping four balls in the air, crisscrossing them, weaving intricate patterns, making each ball drop into place at just the right moment.

A good composer of fugues has many tricks at his disposal. He may break up the subject into parts, turn it upside down (inversion), stretch it out to twice its length (augmentation), or speed it up to double tempo (diminution). While the music turns this way and that, the rhythm moves steadily forward until a high point, or climax, is reached

164

Here the composer often introduces an interesting passage called "stretto," or tightening. In the stretto, all four voices take up the subject in rapid succession. The third voice starts, the second follows quickly, and, without waiting for them to finish, the fourth and the first voices come in, bringing the fugue to a peak of intensity.

Ex. 137d

A few more entrances of the subject, perhaps some further tightening, and the end is reached in that contrapuntal adventure called the fugue.

The composition just described, Fugue No. 1 of the *Well-Tempered Clavier,* like most other fugues, is written in four voices. Fugues are also written in three and in five voices, more rarely for two or six. There are fugues for chorus, as in Handel's *Messiah,* and fugues for orchestra, such as the last movement of Bach's *Brandenburg* Concertos, Nos. 2 and 4. Beethoven wrote a beautiful fugue in the fourth movement of his String Quartet, Op. 59, No. 3, and a brilliant one in the second movement of his Ninth Symphony.

Ex. 138   Beethoven: Symphony No. 9

No form of music is more difficult to describe in words than the fugue, and the discussion given here is no more than the merest introduction to the subject. Fortunately there are other ways of learning about the fugue, and the most important way—as might be suspected by this time—is to listen to fugues, over and over. Besides the opening fugue in the *Well-Tempered Clavier,* I suggest Nos. 2, 5, 6, and 16 in the same collection; the third movement of Bach's *Brandenburg* Concerto No. 2; and the *Little* Fugue in G Minor for Organ. A delightful free fugue is heard in Mozart's Overture to *The Magic Flute,* and interesting, modern ones in the String Quartet No. 3 by Hindemith, and in the Quintet for Piano and Strings by Shostakovich.

Mozart's Favorite Concert Piano and Spinet or Clavichord

Ranges of Instruments

Ex. 139

Chapter 2

—Melodic Curves

Ex. 140   Drink to Me Only with Thine Eyes (Wave)

Drink to me on-ly with thine eyes and I ___ will drink with mine.

Ex. 141   The Minstrel Boy (Rising Wave)

The   min - strel   boy___   to   the   war   has   gone...

Ex. 142   On Top of Old Smoky (Arch)

Way   up   on   old   Smok - y,_____   all   cov-ered with   snow... ___

(Rhythmic Patterns):

Ex. 143   I Dream of Jeanie (Falling Wave)

I   dream   of   Jean - ie   with   the   light   brown   hair...

Ex. 144   Rossini: Overture from *William Tell*

Ex. 145   Jingle Bells

Ex. 146   Beethoven: Symphony No. 5

—*Tone Color* (Orchestration):

1. Flute
2. French Horn
3. Clarinet
4. Timpani
5. Cello and Bass
6. Oboe
7. Violins
8. Trumpet
9. Bassoon
10. Double Basses

—*Two and Three Part Forms:*

"Pop Goes the Weasel"............................Two Part Form
"My Bonnie Lies Over the Ocean"...........Two Part Form
"Old Man River"....................................Three Part Form
"Yankee Doodle"...................................Two Part Form
"Old Folks At Home"............................Three Part Form

10

Building A Record Library

Where there are several recordings of the same work, no recording company is listed.

Folk Music—American

Ballads (Pete Seeger), *Folkways FA 2319*
Negro Folk Music (Sonny Terry), *Folkways FA 2035*
The Old Chisholm Trail (Tony Kraber), *Mercury 20008*
The Rock Island Line (Leadbelly), *Folkways FA 2014*
Smoky Mountain Ballads (Lunsford), *Folkways FA 2040*
Spirituals (Hall and Reed), *Folkways FA 2038*
Talking Dust Bowl (Woody Guthrie), *Folkways FA 2482*
The Wayfaring Stranger (Burl Ives), *Columbia CL 628*

Folk Music—Other Countries

Music of the World's Peoples, *Folkways FE 4504-6*
The World of Man, Work Songs, *Folkways FC 7431*
Africa, Dahomey, *Esoteric ESO 537*
Bali, Gamelan Orchestra, *Westminster XWN 2209*
Bulgarian Folk Music, *Angel 6502 C*
French Folk Songs (Alan Mills), *Folkways FC 7208*
Great British Ballads (McColl and Lloyd), *Riverside 12-629*
Hungary, Bartók Collection, *Westminster XWN 18665*
Irish Jigs, Reels and Hornpipes, *Folkways FW 6818*
Spanish, Cante Flamenco, *Westminster WAP 301*

Classical Composers

BACH

Brandenburg Concertos, Nos. 2 & 3
Coffee Cantata
Concerto in D Minor for Two Violins
Fugue in G Minor for Organ (*Little*)
Peasant Cantata
Suite No. 2 in B Minor for Orchestra
Toccata and Fugue in D Minor for Organ
Two-Part Inventions
Well-Tempered Clavier, Preludes and Fugues Nos. 1, 2, 5, 6, and 16, Book I

BEETHOVEN

Concerto in D Major for Violin and Orchestra
Coriolanus Overture
Egmont Overture
Piano Sonata Op. 13 (*Pathetique*)
Piano Sonata Op. 27 (*Moonlight*)
Piano Sonata Op. 57 (*Appassionata*)
String Quartet Op. 18 No. 1
Symphony No. 3 in E Flat (*Eroica*)
Symphony No. 5 in C Minor
Symphony No. 6 in F (*Pastoral*)
Symphony No. 7 in A
Symphony No. 9 in D Minor (*Choral*)

BERLIOZ

Fantastic Symphony

BIZET

L'Arlésienne Suites, Nos. 1 & 2
Carmen Suite

BORODIN

Polovetsian Dances from *Prince Igor*

BRAHMS

Academic Festival Overture
Concerto in D Major for Violin and Orchestra
Hungarian Dances
Rhapsodies Op. 79
Songs
Symphony No. 2 in D Major
Symphony No. 3 in F Major
Waltzes

CHOPIN

Fantaisie-Impromptu
Mazurkas
Nocturnes
Preludes
Waltzes

DVORAK

Slavonic Dances
Symphony No. 5 in E Minor (*From the New World*)

FOSTER

Songs

GLINKA

Kamarinskaia
Russlan and Ludmilla, Overture

GRIEG

Peer Gynt Suite
Piano Concerto

HANDEL

Concerto in F Major for Organ
Israel in Egypt (Excerpts)
The Messiah (Excerpts)
Water Music Suite

HAYDN

The Creation (Excerpts)
String Quartet in D Minor
Symphony No. 94 (*Surprise*)
Symphony No. 101 (*The Clock*)
Symphony No. 104 (*London*)

LIADOV

Eight Russian Folk Songs

LISZT

Hungarian Rhapsody, No. 2
Les Preludes

MENDELSSOHN

Concerto in E Minor for Violin
Elijah (Excerpts)
A Midsummer Night's Dream
Music
Symphony No. 4 (*Italian*)

MONTEVERDI

Madrigals
"Lament of Arianna"

MORLEY

Elizabethan Madrigals

MOUSSORGSKY

Prelude to *Khovanschina*
A Night on Bald Mountain
Pictures at an Exhibition
Songs

MOZART

Abduction from the Seraglio Over-
ture
Concerto in A Major for Clarinet
Eine Kleine Nachtmusik
German Dances
The Magic Flute Overture
Sonata in A Major for Piano (*K. 331*)
Sonata in C Major for Piano (*K. 545*)
Sonata in E Minor for Violin and
Piano
Symphony No. 35 in D Major
(*Haffner*)
Symphony No. 40 in G Minor
Symphony No. 41 in C Major
(*Jupiter*)

ORLANDO DI LASSO

Chansons and Madrigals

PALESTRINA

Stabat Mater

PURCELL

Dido and Aeneas Orchestral Suite
Trumpet Voluntary

RACHMANINOFF

Piano Concertos Nos. 2 & 3

RIMSKY-KORSAKOFF

Capriccio Espagnol
Le Coq d'Or Suite
Scheherazade Suite

ROSSINI

The Barber of Seville Overture
William Tell Overture

173

SAINT-SAËNS

The Carnival of the Animals
Danse Macabre

SCARLATTI

Sonatas

SCHUBERT

German Dances
Marche Militaire
Moments Musicaux
Quartet No. 14 in D Minor
Rosamunde, Incidental Music
Songs
Symphony No. 8 (*Unfinished*)

SCHUMANN

Fantasy Pieces
Scenes from Childhood
Songs
Symphony No. 1 in B Flat

SIBELIUS

Finlandia
Symphony No. 1 in E Minor

STRAUSS

Don Juan
Till Eulenspiegel's Merry Pranks

TCHAIKOVSKY

"1812" Overture
Nutcracker Suite
Piano Concerto No. 1 in B Flat
   Minor

Romeo and Juliet Overture
Symphony No. 4 in F Minor
Symphony No. 5 in E Minor

VIVALDI

Concerto in A Minor for Violin
Concerto for Two Mandolins
The Seasons

WEBER

Oberon Overture

WOLF

Songs

Opera

BIZET

Carmen (Excerpts)

HUMPERDINCK

Hansel and Gretel (Excerpts)

MENOTTI

Amahl and the Night Visitors
The Medium
The Telephone

MOUSSORGSKY

Boris Godunov (Excerpts)

MOZART

Don Giovanni (Excerpts)
The Magic Flute (Excerpts)
The Marriage of Figaro (Excerpts)

PUCCINI

La Bohème (Excerpts)
Madame Butterfly (Excerpts)
Tosca (Excerpts)

VERDI

Aïda (Excerpts)
Arias (Weede)

174

Overtures and Preludes
La Traviata (Excerpts)
Rigoletto (Excerpts)

WAGNER

Die Meistersinger, Prelude
Die Meistersinger, Dance of the Ap-
prentices from
Die Walküre, The Magic Fire Music
from
Die Walküre, The Ride of the Val-
kyrie from
The Flying Dutchman Overture

The Mastersingers of Nuremberg,
see Die Meistersinger
Siegfried, Forest Murmurs from
Tannhäuser Overture
The Valkyrie, see Die Walküre

WEILL

Down in the Valley

Musical Comedy and Operetta

BERNSTEIN

West Side Story

GILBERT AND SULLIVAN

The Mikado (Excerpts)
Pirates of Penzance (Excerpts)

KERN

Showboat

KLEINSINGER

archy and mehitabel

LANE

Finian's Rainbow

LOESSER

Guys and Dolls

LOEWE

My Fair Lady

OFFENBACH

La Périchole (Excerpts)

PORTER

Kiss Me, Kate

RODGERS

Carousel
The King and I

STRAUSS

Fledermaus, Die (Excerpts)

WEILL

The Three-Penny Opera

Twentieth-Century Composers

BARBER

Adagio for Strings
Medea's Meditation and Dance of
Vengeance

BARTÓK

Allegro Barbaro
Concerto for Orchestra
For Children
Hungarian Folk Songs
Roumanian Dances

BERNSTEIN

Fancy Free

BLOCH

Schelomo

BRITTEN

Young Person's Guide to the Orchestra

COPLAND

Appalachian Spring
El Salon Mexico
A Lincoln Portrait
Rodeo

DEBUSSY

The Afternoon of a Faun
Children's Corner Suite
Clair de Lune
Ibéria No. 2 from *Images* for Or-
chestra
Nocturnes

DUKAS

The Sorcerer's Apprentice

GERSHWIN

An American in Paris
Concerto in F
Porgy and Bess (Excerpts)
Rhapsody in Blue

GOULD

Interplay
Latin-American Symphonette
Pavane

HINDEMITH

Kleine Kammermusik Op. 24 No. 1
Symphonic Metamorphosis on
Themes by Weber

HONEGGER

Chant de Joie (Song of Joy)
Pacific 231

IVES

Sonata No. 1 for Violin and Piano
Sonata No. 2 for Violin and Piano
Songs
The Unanswered Question

KODALY

Háry János Suite

MILHAUD

Le Boeuf sur le Toit
The Creation of the World
Suite Française

MOORE

Farm Journal

POULENC

Babar the Elephant
Mouvements Perpétuels

PROKOFIEV

Alexander Nevsky
Classical Symphony in D Major
Concerto No. 1 in D Major, for
    Violin and Orchestra
Concerto No. 3 in C Major, for
    Piano and Orchestra
Lieutenant Kijé Suite
Love for Three Oranges March
Overture on Hebrew Themes
Peter and the Wolf
Symphony No. 5, Op. 100

RAVEL

Boléro
Daphnis and Chloë
Introduction and Allegro
Mother Goose Suite
Pavane
Tzigane

REVUELTAS

Music of Revueltas
Ochos por Radio

SHOSTAKOVICH

Concerto No. 1 for Piano
Quintet for Piano and Strings
Symphony No. 1 in F Minor
Symphony No. 5, Op. 47

SIEGMEISTER

Ozark Set
Sunday in Brooklyn

STRAVINSKY

The Fire Bird Suite
Petroushka Suite
The Rite of Spring
The Story of a Soldier (RCA Victor)

THOMSON

Acadian Songs and Dances
Louisiana Story
The Plow that Broke the Plains

TOCH

The Chinese Flute
Symphony No. 3, Op. 75

VAUGHAN-WILLIAMS

Fantasia on *Greensleeves*
Fantasia on a Theme by Tallis
Suite, *English Folk Songs*

VILLA-LOBOS

Bachianas Brasileiras No. 5 for So-
    prano and Celli
Little Train of the Caipira
Origin of the Amazon River
Uirapurú

Jazz Recordings

The best introductions to jazz on a single LP are:

Leonard Bernstein, "What is Jazz," *Columbia 919*
Langston Hughes, "The Story of Jazz," *Folkways FC 7312*

The finest overall coverage of the growth of jazz is to be found in:

Folkways Jazz Series, Vols. 1-11, *Nos. 2801-11*

Other surveys of jazz include:

Encyclopedia of Jazz, *Decca DL 8398-41*
History of Jazz, *Capitol T793-6*
History of Classic Jazz, vols. 1-5, *Riverside SDP 11*

For the early period of jazz, listen to:

The Bessie Smith Story, *Columbia CL 855-8*
King Oliver, *Epic LN 3208*
Satchmo, a Musical Autobiography, *Decca DXM 155*
The Louis Armstrong Story, *Columbia CL 851-4*
The Great Sixteen! (Muggsy Spanier's Ragtime Band), *RCA Victor LPM 1295*
Bunk Johnson, *ML 4802*
Lady Day (Billie Holiday), *Columbia CL 637*
Lou Watters' Yerba Buena Jazz Band, *Good Time Jazz GTJL 1200-3*
Count Basie, *Brunswick BL 54012*
Sidney Bechet Jazz Classics, *Blue Note BLP 1201-2*
The Bix Beiderbecke Story, *Columbia CL 844-6*
Chicago Style Jazz, *Columbia CL 632*

For the jazz of the '30s and early '40s, see:

The Music of Duke Ellington, *Columbia CL 558*
Ellington Uptown, *Columbia ML 4639*
The King of Swing (Benny Goodman), *Columbia CL 817-9*
Bijou (Woody Herman), *Harmony HL 7013*

Outstanding records of more recent jazz include:

Birth of the Cool (Miles Davis), *Capitol 762*
The Kenton Era, *Capital WDX 569*
The Charlie Parker Story, *Verve 8000-2*
Jazz West Coast, *JWC 500-1*
The Modern Jazz Quartet, *Atlantic 1265*
The Unique Thelonius Monk, *Riverside RLP 12-209*
The Gerry Mulligan Quartet, *Pacific Jazz PJ-1228*

Instruments of the Orchestra

The Complete Orchestra (Wheeler Beckett) *Music Education Records 1-5*
The First Chair, *Columbia ML 4629*
Young Person's Guide to the Orchestra (Britten)

11

Books About Music

*Indicates paperback edition

The Materials of Music—How to Listen

Boyden, David D., *An Introduction to Music,* Alfred A. Knopf, Inc., New York, 1956.

*Copland, Aaron, *What to Listen for in Music,* McGraw-Hill Book Co., Inc., New York, 1957 (rev. ed.).

Dorian, Frederick, *The Musical Workshop,* Harper & Brothers, New York, 1947.

Machlis, Joseph, *The Enjoyment of Music,* W. W. Norton & Co., Inc., New York, 1955.

*Salter, Lionel, *Going to a Concert,* Penguin, Harmondsworth, England, 1950.

*Salter, Lionel, *Going to the Opera,* Penguin, Harmondsworth, England, 1955.

Siegmeister, Elie, *The Music Lover's Handbook,* William Morrow & Co., Inc., New York, 1955.

Ulrich, Homer, *A Design for Listening,* Harcourt, Brace & Co., New York, 1957.

Folk Music

Boni, Margaret Bradford, and Lloyd, Norman, *Fireside Book of Folk Songs,* Simon and Shuster, Inc., New York, 1947.

Downes, Olin, and Siegmeister, Elie, *A Treasury of American Song,* Alfred A. Knopf, Inc., New York, 1943.

*Ives, Burl, *The Burl Ives Song Book,* Ballantine Books, Houghton Mifflin Co., Boston, 1953.

179

*Kolb, Sylvia and John, *A Treasury of Folk Songs,* Bantam Books, New York, 1948.

Lomax, John and Alan, *Folk Song: U. S. A.,* Duell, Sloan & Pearce, Inc., New York, 1947.

Sandburg, Carl, *The American Songbag,* Harcourt, Brace & Co., New York, 1927.

Great Works of Music

Bagar, Robert, and Biancolli, Louis, *The Concert Companion,* McGraw-Hill Book Co., Inc., New York, 1947.

*Dent, Edward J., *Opera,* Penguin, Harmondsworth, England, 1949.

*Hill, Ralph, *The Symphony,* Penguin, Harmondsworth, England, 1949.

*Newman, Ernest, *Great Operas,* Vols. 1-2, Vintage Books, Alfred A. Knopf, Inc., New York, 1958.

Seaman, Julius, *Great Orchestral Music,* Rinehart & Co., Inc., New York, 1950.

*Shaw, Bernard, *Shaw on Music,* Anchor Book, Doubleday & Co., Inc., New York, 1955.

Ulrich, Homer, *Chamber Music,* Columbia University Press, New York, 1948.

Ulrich, Homer, *Symphonic Music,* Columbia University Press, New York, 1952.

General Reference and History

Apel, Willi, *Harvard Dictionary of Music,* Harvard University Press, Cambridge, Massachusetts, 1950.

Becker, Paul, *The Story of Music,* W. W. Norton & Co., Inc., New York, 1927.

Davis, Marilyn, and Broido, Arnold, *Music Dictionary,* Doubleday & Co., Inc., New York, 1956 (rev. ed.).

*Einstein, Alfred, *A Short History of Music,* Vintage Book, Alfred A. Knopf, Inc., New York, 1954.

Scholes, Percy, *Junior Oxford Companion to Music,* Oxford University Press, New York, 1954.

The Great Composers

*Bacharach, A. L., *The Music Masters,* Vols. 1-4, Penguin, Harmondsworth, England, 1957.

Biancolli, Louis, and Peyser, Herbert, *Masters of the Orchestra,* G. P. Putnam's Sons, New York, 1954.

*Brockway, Wallace, and Weinstock, Herbert, *Men of Music,* Simon and Schuster, Inc., New York, 1958.

Ewen, David, *From Bach to Stravinsky,* W. W. Norton & Co., Inc., New York, 1933.

Morgenstern, Sam, *Composers on Music,* Pantheon Books, Inc., New York, 1956.

Twentieth-Century Music

Abraham, Gerald, *This Modern Music,* W. W. Norton & Co., Inc., New York, 1952.

Copland, Aaron, *Our New Music,* McGraw-Hill Book Co., Inc., New York, 1941.

*Cohn, Arthur, *The Collector's Twentieth Century Music in the Western Hemisphere,* J. B. Lippincott Co., Philadelphia, 1961.

Ewen, David, *The Book of Modern Composers,* Alfred A. Knopf, Inc., New York, 1942.

Ewen, David, *The Complete Book of 20th Century Music,* Prentice-Hall, Inc., New York, 1952.

*Hartog, Howard, *European Music in the Twentieth Century,* Frederick A. Praeger, New York, 1957.

*Howard, John T., and Lyons, James, *Modern Music,* Mentor Books, New American Library of World Literature, Inc., New York, 1957.

*Lambert, Constant, *Music Ho!,* Penguin, Harmondsworth, England, 1948.

Jazz

*Armstrong, Louis, *Satchmo,* Mentor Books, New American Library of World Literature, Inc., New York, 1956.

Hughes, Langston, *The First Book of Jazz,* Franklin Watts, Inc., New York, 1954.

*Stearns, Marshall W., *The Story of Jazz,* Mentor Books, New American Library of World Literature, Inc., New York, 1958.

12

Index

A A B A form, 52-56
A B form, 55-57
A B A form, 52, 55, 56
A B A C A D A form, 60; *see also* rondo
Academic Festival Overture, Brahms, *9
A cappella, 71
Accelerando, 36
Accents, 28, 35
Adagio, 36
Afterbeat, 88
Afternoon of a Faun, The, Debussy, 47, 91, *135
Africa, 3; and the blues scale, 147; music in, 3; rhythm of, 33
Aida, Verdi, 79, 130
Alexander Nevsky, Prokofiev, 73, 83, 139
Allargando, 36
Allegretto, 36
Allegro, 36
Alto saxophone, 167
Amahl and the Night Visitors, Menotti, 80
America, *53-54
America, music of, *145-156;* cowboy ballads, 145; folk songs, 8-10, 145; Mississippi boatmen songs, 145; musical comedy, *80-82;* opera, 79-80; popular songs, 147, 150, 152; ragtime, 145, 149; railroad songs, 145; rhythms, 35; sentimental songs of the '90s, 145; *see also* jazz, American songs
American in Paris, An, Gershwin, 143
Andante, 36
Anderson, Maxwell, 82
  Lost in the Stars, 82
Animando, 36
Appalachian Spring, Copland, 84, 144
Appassionata Sonata, Op. 57, Beethoven, 62
Aria, 77-79
Arlen, Harold, 150
Armstrong, Louis, 147, 149
Art of Fugue, Bach, 115, 134
Art song, 74-75; *see also* Lieder and the Song Cycle
Atonality, 133
Au Clair de la Lune, *22
Augmentation, 164

Babylon, 3; music in ancient, 3
Bach, Johann Sebastian, 27, 107, *115-16,* 138, 155; and the cantata, 72; and the concerto, 68; and the fugue, 32, 45, *163-66;* and the suite, 58
  Art of Fugue, 115, 134
  B Minor Mass, 71 ,115
  Brandenburg Concertos, *114, 165, 166
  Coffee Cantata, 72
  Concerto No. 3 in D Minor for Two Violins, *23, *115
  Fugue No. 1, Well-Tempered Clavier, *163-66
  Fugues Nos. 2, 5, 6, and 16, Well-Tempered Clavier, 166
  Little Fugue in G Minor for Organ, 166

183

184

185

186

187

189

190

192

193